Buttercup

Buttercup

The Legendary Charm and Love of a Domestic Short-Haired Tabby Cat

Jerome Tonneson

BLB
PRESS

Lenexa, Kansas

Copyright © 2013 Jerome Tonneson

All rights reserved. This book contains material protected under international and Federal Copyright Treaties. Any unauthorized reprint or use of this material is prohibited. No part of this book may be reproduced or transmitted in any form or by any means, electronic or mechanical, including photocopying, recording, or by information storage and retrieval system without express written permission from the publisher.

Published by BLB Press
blb-press.com

Photo credits:
Pages 8, 35, and 173: Ronald Tonneson. Page 17: Darek Benesh.
All other interior and exterior photos provided by the author.

Paperback ISBN: 978-0-9891242-0-1
Hardback ISBN: 978-0-9891242-1-8

Library of Congress Control Number: 2013908251
Library of Congress subject headings:
Cats—Biography
Cats—Anecdotes
Human-animal relationships

1.3

To Cat Lovers Everywhere

Contents

Foreword..3

Introduction...5

Chapter 1: Meet Buttercup...........................9

Chapter 2: Remarkable Beauty..................17

Chapter 3: Dinnertime...............................23

Chapter 4: Quench a Thirst, Feline-Style...35

Chapter 5: Playtime...................................45

Chapter 6: A Body at Rest.........................57

Chapter 7: Bedtime Stories........................69

Chapter 8: Behavior...................................87

Chapter 9: The Problem-Solving Kitty......99

Chapter 10: It's Good to be Queen...........123

Chapter 11: Cat Tales...............................131

Chapter 12: On the Prowl........................149

Chapter 13: Unquestioned Love..............173

Epilogue...191

Acknowledgments...................................195

Buttercup

Foreword

At the Cat Clinic of Johnson County, we were very fortunate to have provided "Buttercup" Tonneson's veterinary care for most of her life. We first saw her in 1999 when she was approximately two years old, and continued to see her regularly throughout the years.

She had her share of the more common ailments, such as allergies and bladder infections, which she handled with quiet reserve. She was never thrilled about her visits, or the medication we charged her poor human with administering to her, but came to allow the insults gracefully.

I've always said that cats are more like people in that some will just give up in the face of adversity, while others will fight with every ounce of strength they have left.

Buttercup was one of the fighters. She had such a will to live that even at the end of her life she was determined to continue her usual behaviors. Her bond with Jerome was, I'm sure, a big part of her strong will to live.

I will always remember her sweet face, her beautiful coat, and most importantly, that soul-to-soul connection she had with the person who gave her the love and the life she so deserved.

Dr. Irene Schomacker, DVM

Introduction

Moments after I sat down at the computer, she jumped into my lap, circled once, then lay down to settle in for an evening of snuggling. Her striped tail draped across my leg while she reached up toward my left hand, pulled it down to my lap, demanding I place it where she could rest her chin on my wrist. Thus began another typical evening.

Any animal lover will tell you that pets aren't just animals. Like people, each is a unique being with his or her own complex personality. It is the combination of that personality and the accumulation of experiences and knowledge that defines the creature. What follows is a collection of humorous anecdotes, quirky behaviors, and heart-warming stories that characterized one extraordinarily simple house cat. Cat lovers especially will likely relate to many of these stories.

It's been said that cats are not very social creatures—that they are aloof or uppity. There's a joke that goes something like this: A dog thinks to himself, "My human pets me and plays with me and feeds me and loves me—he must be God!" Whereas the cat thinks, "My human pets me and plays with me and feeds me and loves me—he must think I'm God!" A dog will befriend just about anyone, but a cat's friendship and trust will be bestowed upon only those who have earned it. Ask most anyone who has been around cats for any length of time and that person probably tell you that cats do in fact develop very intricate relationships with both humans and other cats, but only when the relationships are merited.

Buttercup was with me for nearly fourteen years of her sixteen-year life. I knew losing her was going to be difficult, but I tried not to think about it. After all, she wasn't losing sleep over her eventual passing, so why should I? A cat knows when she is dying, but until that day comes, she doesn't worry about it. I tried to live by that same philosophy by enjoying every moment I could with her. There were many times when she was comfortably sleeping on my lap and I wanted to get up for some reason, but I chose to remain still. I would only disturb her in exceptional cases. Later in her life when I knew the end was near, I tried to remember all the good times—her funny behaviors, her unique quirks, her loving nature, her intelligence, and the unbelievable things she did during her life. This book is a collection of all those great things that made Buttercup uniquely Buttercup. As time passes, memories will fade and details will slip into ambiguity. Writing about her life is a way to preserve her memory, something that my future self will appreciate.

Although this collection of stories is primarily about Buttercup, she and I did not live in isolation. Throughout these stories, you also will come across a few other cats and people who came into Buttercup's life.

Buttercuppy

Chapter 1: Meet Buttercup

Buttercup came into my life by chance. I was living in an apartment when my parents came to visit one autumn weekend. Apparently not enamored with the thought of sleeping on my sofa or floor, my parents instead stayed with some friends—a very nice retired couple, Don and Martha "Marty" Mather. The Mathers were kind enough to invite me over to have breakfast with them and my parents. The Mathers had three cats, a rabbit, and a dog that would get excited and smile whenever someone took out a camera. The cats included an exotic purebred male, a Siamese female, and a plain brown mackerel tabby female.

The tabby had come from a shelter approximately one year before, and at the time was estimated to be less than a year old. The Mathers' granddaughter, Adrienne, who was approximately six years old, decided to name her "Buttercup." Marty would later comment that she didn't know where Adrienne came up with that wonderful name.

Buttercup was to be a gift for one of the Mathers' granddaughters; however, something happened that prevented that from taking place. As such, Buttercup stayed with the Mathers and took on the job of greeting and caring for their frequent guests. During that time, Marty had been trying to find a home for her. The first time I met her, she offered Buttercup to me. At first, I thought she was joking but the next day she repeated the offer. Unfortunately, I was not able to take her easily, since I was living in an apartment that did not cater to pets.

A few months later, I purchased my first house. Closing was on November 25, the day before Thanksgiving. I spent the next few weeks taking care of a few things around the house and moving items from my apartment. Since I didn't really know anyone in the area and my family was a few hundred miles away, I moved nearly everything by myself. I actually preferred this approach, since it permitted the move to happen in a controlled fashion rather than the single-day chaos that most people endure. By mid December, I was ready to start living in the house.

A few weeks later, on December 28, I called Marty to see if the offer to take Buttercup was still valid. She said "yes" and that I could pick her up any time that day. I wasn't feeling well, as I was starting to come down with what seemed like a cold, but I decided I felt well enough that I could go pick up a new pet. After a trip to a pet-supply store, I made the trek over to the Mathers' house.

Buttercup moved into my house just two weeks after I did. I read somewhere that a house is not a home until there is a cat living there. This certainly seemed true. Now when I left work, instead of returning to a cold, lifeless building, I was going to a warm, loving home where someone was there to greet me.

There was an adjustment period for Buttercup when she moved in. This house was only about a third the size of her previous residence. After some unsupervised roaming—which most cats require when exploring a new place—she hunted me down, cocked her head slightly, and looked at me as if to ask, *Where's the rest of it?* This house didn't have a large sunroom like her previous one did, or a large basement, or an expansive upper floor.

Most disturbingly, though, was that she seemed to be looking for her feline friends. During the first few weeks, she would often sit at the end of the hallway and call for them. When she did this, I felt guilty for taking her away from those she loved. When she spent time with me, she seemed happy, so at least that made me feel a little better. After a few weeks, she became accustomed to being the only cat in the house and I think even enjoyed having sole control over this entire new territory. I did feel sorry for her, though, when I went off to work. I wondered what she did all day, although I figured that being a cat, she mostly slept. After all, cats need plenty of rest to recover from all the eating and napping they do. Less than three years later, Buttercup received a feline companion in the form of a domestic, long-haired, dilute tortoiseshell named Lily.

Lily joined the family when she was approximately three months old. She came from a coworker who lived in the country. For some strange reason, he did not permit cats in the house. This, of course, was incomprehensible to me. Cats, after all, are living sculptures; they're fine works of art. How can you have a home without one? Anyway, his family recently had had two cats that were permitted in the garage but mostly lived outside. They both had tragically short lives as many outdoor cats do. Soon after that, another kitten showed up at their door and began the life of a garage cat. One of my coworker's sons named this little female cat "Lily."

A couple of months later, as my coworker was getting ready to leave for work, he couldn't find Lily in the garage. He got in his truck and drove down the 600-foot long driveway. Soon after turning onto the two-lane county highway, he saw a bundle of fur fly out of one of the wheel wells. He stopped and searched but couldn't locate her. Later that day, his kids found her in the field. She had survived the incident with superficial injuries. Later he told his kids that Lily was more likely to have a long and happy life if she could live in a house in the city. The following Sunday afternoon, I went to pick her up.

I took Lily to the Cat Clinic of Johnson County for a checkup, shots, and spaying. The only thing the veterinarian noticed was something stuck in Lily's fur under her chin—something that I speculated was dried blood from the truck incident. The vet declared Lily to be in good health.

The vet warned me, though, that tortoiseshells, or "torties" as they are often called, can be a bit obnoxious—her exact word. This turned out to be true. Lily was very emotional and opinionated, and not at all shy about revealing her thoughts. She was very sweet, but also extremely playful and quite talkative. She didn't like to travel and would make that point very clear. Whenever she was due for a checkup, I joked that the folks at the Cat Clinic could hear us coming a mile away thanks to Lily's howling.

Lily was supposed to keep Buttercup company. It was nice for Buttercup to have someone to play with while I was at work. While Lily did a good job of that, there were times when her attention was a bit too intense. I often thought that perhaps there needed to be a *third* cat so that Lily's energy and antics could be divided among them, thus giving Buttercup some relief. Then I wondered, *Where would it end?* How many cats are needed to reach equilibrium? The answer, at least in this case, was three. I discovered that a couple of years later when Bubba joined the household.

Unlike Lily, Bubba was much more subdued, as male cats frequently are. Some kids playing in the dry creek behind my neighbor's house found him. The next day, my neighbors checked the creek again and saw that he was still there. They took him in and cleaned him up, but they had a dog and didn't think that bringing a cat into the house would work very well. They also knew that I already had cats and therefore cat supplies, so they brought him over to me.

Bubba was a gorgeous kitten. He had black and brown marble classic tabby markings on his sides. His paws and belly consisted of the brightest white fur I had ever seen. His white fur was so brilliant and was easy to spot in the dark that I referred to him as my "glow-in-the-dark" kitty. The white fur also formed a band around his neck, a tiny spot on his back, and a bright blaze on his nose highlighted with a couple of brown spots.

I left him quarantined in the basement, as I had done with Lily, to help him and the other cats adjust to each other. Plus, he hadn't yet been tested for feline leukemia or FIV.

He was very sweet and not afraid of people at all, so I figured he must have a family. I put signs up in the neighborhood and waited for a phone call that never came. After a week, I took him to the Cat Clinic for a checkup.

He was quite young and too underdeveloped to be tested for contagious diseases, so he remained quarantined for nearly a month. Other than that, the clinic said he appeared to be in good health except for having an empty belly. I hadn't named him yet because I wasn't even sure if he was a "he." This kitten was so underdeveloped that even the trained vet tech didn't feel comfortable making the call. When Dr. Schomacker walked into the examination room and saw him exploring along the far wall, she knew what she was looking at. Without even picking him up she said, "He's a boy. And he's going to be a big boy!"

Later during the examination, she called him "Bubba." The name stuck, and she was right: that adorable little kitten grew to become a large, incredibly handsome cat with soft, shiny, and silky fur. He was very strong and muscular but extremely gentle. His powerful hind legs could propel great leaps, yet he'll reach out and touch me softly.

Despite several sleepless nights while raising both of these kittens, Buttercup enjoyed having them around and sharing her house with them.

Sunbeam at the Basement Door

Chapter 2: Remarkable Beauty

Buttercup was a domestic short-haired cat. In other words, an ordinary house cat. Contrary to this simple characterization, she had a striking beauty. There was a certain elegance in her simplicity.

The word "tabby" does not refer to a breed of cat, but rather the markings of the coat. A tabby will have stripes, dots, or a marbled swirling pattern, with fur in a variety of colors. Though she had practically no brown fur, Buttercup's coloring and markings officially made her a "brown mackerel tabby." Due to her gray fur, it could be argued that she was more of a silver tabby than a brown tabby. Buttercup's soft tail consisted of alternating black and silver bands culminating in a solid black tip. Nearly every strand of her coat was black with a single white band. Magically, hundreds of thousands of those strands combined to form a remarkable black and silver pattern of stripes on her back, sides, paws, and tail. Her small, round, kitten-like face was adorned with a classic black "M" tabby marking above her wide, pale-green eyes. She groomed her fur meticulously, and often received additional cleaning from the other cats. Her fur was so soft that at times I could barely feel it when rubbing her neck or behind her ears. Over time, her darker whiskers faded to white. Her immaculately clean ears were always on, monitoring her surroundings and picking up sounds I couldn't hear.

Most people who met her noticed her simple beauty. Everyone at her veterinary office, the Cat Clinic of Johnson County, would comment on how pretty she was. People would especially notice the silkiness of her shiny coat—a sign that she was happy, proud, and took very good care of herself. This was fortunate for me, since Buttercup was not very fond of being brushed. She would tolerate it, but I could tell it annoyed her. When I brushed her, she would often complain softly to me, and if I didn't listen to her, she'd sneak away from me. Despite being a lap cat, if I got the brush out, she would often decide that lap time was over. In her later years, she would hide behind the computer's LCD monitor, where she knew I couldn't easily reach her. Luckily, she really only needed a little help with her coat a couple of times a year during late spring and summer.

Part of the reason why she rarely needed to be brushed was that she was quite capable of shedding. Most of her fur ended up on me. I would stroke her back as she settled in on my lap, sometimes for over an hour at a time. Often my shirts and pants ended up covered in fur. There was fur everywhere! On the bed, on the floor, on the sofa, in the cat trees, on my chair. I'd find fur in the oddest places. I'd pick up a strand and inspect it. Black with one white band. Yep, that's Buttercup's fur. Even opening up a kitchen cupboard to pull out a clean bowl or cup I'd find Buttercup's fur. *How did she do that? I just cleaned those cups!* There were times when I'd wake up in the morning after Buttercup and Lily spent the night with me; I'd feel something not quite right and reach up to my tongue. Cat fur! What were those girls doing to me in the middle of the night? How were they giving me hairballs?

Fur would even end up on my chair at work. My employer had "take your child to work" days but never a "take your cat to work day." Yet, somehow, I'd find Buttercup fur on my lab bench and office chair. Personally, I think "take your cat to work day" would have been much more enjoyable, even if it increased the amount of fur in the office. Buttercup liked to travel and probably would have enjoyed it.

Buttercup was always taking care of her fur. She was one of the licking-est cats I've ever seen. Cats want to be clean, and she was definitely a perfectionist in that regard. Apparently, the ideal time for a bath was about five minutes after I went to bed. Just as I'd be settling in with her curled up next to me, she'd start in on her bathing routine. From head to tail, she'd clean her face, belly, back, all four paws, plus the unmentionable areas. Once satisfied that she was as clean as a cat could be, she'd readjust her position on the bed and get some rest.

Another ideal place for a bath was on my lap. Again, she'd start about five minutes after getting comfy, and often trustingly lean against my hand or arm to support herself while her tongue went for those hard-to-reach places. Sometimes she'd even decide that I needed a feline bath. One day was particularly memorable. As she was cleaning herself, lick after lick, she moved on to my hand without hesitation. She worked her way all the way up my arm to my elbow before deciding that I was clean enough.

Quite by accident, one day after getting out of the shower, I discovered an incredible grooming method that she loved. She was walking around on the bathroom sink, rubbing herself all over me. Apparently, I didn't smell right coming out of the shower, so she needed to re-mark me as her property. My skin was still a bit damp as I started to pet her. I noticed that more of her loose fur seemed to end up on my hands than normal but as my hands dried, the fur removal tapered off to the normal, slightly annoying level. Being the scientific type, I decided to perform an experiment. I wet my hands in the sink again and lightly dried them to about the level of moisture they were at when I began petting her. Once again, loose fur started to fly off her as I stroked her back and sides. There seemed to be an ideal level of moisture for grooming. Too little water had no effect while too much just resulted in a wet cat. The right level of moisture made my hands more effective than any of the half dozen or so cat-grooming tools I'd purchased over the years.

The best part, though, was that unlike all of those grooming tools, Buttercup absolutely loved this form of grooming! She would pace back and forth in front of me, rubbing against me and wrapping her tail around me, lapping up all the attention she could. Soon, the marbled, almond-colored sink took on a speckled gray hue as she shed fur all over it. Once she was done, I had a bit of a chore cleaning up all of the loose fur, but it was worth it to have a well-groomed and happy cat.

Having slightly moistened hands also helped reduce the buildup of static electricity. Unlike the other cats, Buttercup's fur seemed particularly prone to static discharge, especially during the drier times of the year. Receiving a shock was not pleasant for either of us, but she didn't seem bothered by it. I think she was smart enough to know that I wasn't doing it intentionally. Perhaps the pleasure of the gentle stroking and assisted grooming outweighed the occasional zap. Regardless, when I gave her attention, I did my best to be mindful of static discharge.

Buttercup was never a large cat, but for a few years in her prime, she would not have been considered small. A noticeable characteristic was her plush, low-hanging belly. One of the veterinarians at the Cat Clinic, Dr. Bonnie Dechant, was starting to worry about Buttercup's weight. She hoped Buttercup would lose a little weight, or at the very least, not gain any more. During the next checkup, Dr. Dechant was pleased to see that Buttercup had lost a little bit of weight, but she still had to comment on that belly—and coined a new term in the process. "Her weight is good, although she's still a bit…Buttercuppy."

From that day on, I had one word to describe Buttercup's physique. I've always wondered about that belly, though. Did she have kittens at one point? She didn't while she lived with me or with the Mathers, and I think before then she was too young. But I don't know anything about her life before she lived with the Mathers, and she kept those secrets securely locked away in her feline mind. She certainly would have made a wonderful mother cat.

Chapter 3: Dinnertime

Cats don't eat doughnuts, right? They're carnivores. They eat meat and fish. So I figured there should be no problem if I left a box of Hostess chocolate doughnuts on the kitchen table. I'd opened it for breakfast but folded the lid back down to preserve freshness as much as possible. When I arrived home that evening, I found the lid pried open. One of the doughnuts had a small bite taken out of it. Buttercup was my only roommate at the time, so she couldn't pin it on anyone else. Fortunately, she didn't acquire a taste for chocolate doughnuts since they certainly are not the healthiest thing for a cat to eat. They're not the healthiest thing for me to eat either, but that's a different story.

Speaking of unhealthy foods, how about McDonald's french fries? Anyone who has ordered fast food knows about the wonderful treat of "bag fries"—the french fries at the bottom of the bag after everyone has removed his or her order. One Saturday for lunch, I stopped by McDonald's and ordered a typical burger-and-fries meal to go. After arriving home and flipping the TV on, I dug into the bag. As I removed the burger and sleeve of fries, I noticed a lone bag fry, but I left it, setting the bag on the floor. While I ate, Buttercup poked her head into the bag. She was a cat, so she was curious about everything, and I figured she was just checking things out and wouldn't bother the french fry. Seconds later, I saw her head pop out of the bag with the french fry clenched between her jaws and a determined yet satisfied look on her face. She took a few steps back and dropped the fry while I returned my attention to the TV. A bit later, I looked around and saw that the fry was gone; she had eaten the whole thing. But who could blame her? After all, who doesn't like McDonald's french fries?

It turned out she was a bit of a fry snob. She only liked McDonald's french fries. When offered other brands, she would just sniff them and then turn her nose up at them.

Throughout her life, I would occasionally give her a french fry as a treat. Frequently she would eat it, but other times she'd pass on it and turn her attention to the tasty meat on my sandwich. When she was an only cat, she was very polite. If she deemed that I was eating something worthwhile, she would patiently wait for me to give her a bite. Once she received her nibble, she was satisfied and would proceed on her way. All that changed once Lily moved in.

When Lily was younger, she was a rather rotund kitty. I tried to tell people that she was just fluffy due to all of her long hair. Her fur was so long that she had trouble cleaning her neck and chest—she'd run out of tongue before reaching the ends of the strands. No one bought it, though. Lily was fat. Lily was also very interested in whatever I was eating. Unlike Buttercup, she wouldn't leave after receiving her bite even though she would normally only get one. She also taught this to Buttercup. Soon, whenever I ate, I had two cats staring at me intently. One was patiently waiting for a bite and the other was not so patiently waiting.

Surprisingly, Lily was the more patient one. As Buttercup aged, she became more aggressive with my food. (Perhaps "persistent" is a better term.) Soon, she would even reach for my plate. The expression on her face was adorable: she seemed to ignore me completely and instead focused on whatever tasty morsels were on my plate. More than once, she tugged my plate before I could stop her, but I always managed to recover my meal before she got to it. If she couldn't reach my plate from one angle, she would try another. If I was on the sofa she'd approach from one side, and when that didn't work, she'd jump onto the back of the sofa and walk around my head and approach from behind. Or, she'd walk onto the sofa arm to see if that might get her closer to my plate. I always had to be on guard whenever I ate: not only was she persistent, she was also silent and very quick.

Buttercup's persistence at dinnertime also entertained my parents. Being single, I rarely ate at the table. Instead, I normally ate on the sofa while watching TV or I would take my plate to my hobby room. So, for me to eat at the table was a bit of a strange sight for Buttercup. When my parents visited, we would have a more traditional meal sitting at the kitchen table, but this certainly didn't stop Buttercup from checking things out. She would jump into my lap, raise her head, and sniff toward my plate. I would slide my chair back or move my plate as necessary to keep her nose away from it. Sometimes I would give her a bite, just as I did when I ate alone. A few times, I even let her lick the plate after I was done while she was still sitting on my lap. We had to be careful when getting the meal ready, as Buttercup would frequently jump onto one of the chairs and start to inspect whatever we were placing on the table.

Her food aggressiveness wasn't just limited to me. One autumn, a pet sitter experienced it while I went on a weeklong trip to the high desert of Nevada.

One of my hobbies is high-power rocketry. For anyone interested in that hobby, mecca is the Black Rock Desert in Nevada. Each fall, it is the site of a three-day launch of the largest and most powerful amateur rockets in the world. It's quite a drive to get there, but I was working with a few other folks on a project and needed to be there to support them. Due to the length of the trip, I hired a pet sitter to check up on my feline family while I was away. This worked out well, and of course, the cats behaved exactly opposite to the manner in which I said they would. I figured Buttercup wouldn't have time to be bothered by guests, and Lily would hide, while Bubba would come out for some attention. Rather, Bubba hid and Buttercup came out to check up on the pet sitter. The sitter, Pat, was very good at her job. She not only took care of the essentials but she also spent time with the cats. One day she brought some ice cream to eat while socializing with them. She later reported that while Bubba was a no-show, the girls hovered over her like vultures while she ate her ice cream. I had never really considered that, but it was the perfect analogy. Every time I ate, both Buttercup and Lily would keep a very close eye on my food, just waiting for an opportunity to move in if I let my guard down. Buttercup, especially, would try to find her way to a high spot so she could get the upper paw and look down on me.

For economic reasons, I purchased dry cat food in large bags. Normally, I bought at least two varieties because the cats were different ages and had different dietary needs. Rather than keeping the food in the bags where it would become stale, I always transferred it to a set of sealed containers. In order to mix the food, I poured the bags into the containers in multiple passes. First, I would open all of the containers and lay them out in a line on the kitchen floor.

I'd dump part of the first bag into each container, followed by part of the second bag, then back to the first. I did this until all of the food was transferred.

The girls were always there to supervise this activity. Food fresh from the bag tasted better than the food that had been sitting out in their bowls all day. As I poured the food into each tall container, both Buttercup and Lily would decide they needed to take samples. Buttercup more than once stepped into a container with her front paws in order to reach for a bite. Another method they used was to grab a mouthful and dump it on the floor. This quality-control process meant that transferring the food took longer than it should have, since I had to time the pours to avoid dumping food on various cat heads, but at least when I was done I knew they were satisfied that the food stores were in good shape.

Each cat that moved into my house received a matching set of food and water dishes. These were stainless steel dishes that hung from a stainless steel rack. I placed the first set in the kitchen against the wall adjacent to the living room, with the food bowl on the left and water on the right. While standing at the food bowl, the cat could easily see into the living room. When the next cat arrived, I placed her bowls to the right of the first set.

I noticed that whenever only one cat was eating, she always chose the left-most bowl. If both cats were eating, they would normally use separate bowls although occasionally they would attempt to share a single dish. When Bubba moved in and I added the third set of bowls to the right of the others, he also seemed to prefer eating from the far-left bowl. It's not clear why that one was the most desirable, but I suspect it had something to do with the proximity of the living room. From that location, they could eat while keeping an eye on whatever was happening in both the kitchen and living room, giving them more options for a safe escape route if one became necessary.

Concerning these bowls, I did not appreciate how neat and tidy Buttercup was until Lily moved in. Part of my morning routine was to wash and refill Buttercup's food and water dishes. Occasionally I would wipe down the floor near the bowls, but there wasn't a need to do that on a regular basis, as Buttercup rarely made a mess. That all changed when Lily joined us. When I added the second set of food and water dishes, there should have only been twice as much cleaning, but somehow the amount of cleaning went up significantly. Now there was food everywhere—on the floor in the kitchen, on the floor in the living room, even floating in the water bowls. They were like *The Odd Couple*—Buttercup was very orderly while Lily was a complete slob.

Despite Lily's messiness, Buttercup did her best to maintain a clean house. Not only did she wash herself religiously, she would wash the other cats and clean up after them. I might stroll through the kitchen on a Saturday evening and see a bit of dry food floating in one of the water bowls, but when I washed the dish the following morning, the piece would be gone. Occasionally, Buttercup did not clean up after Lily and I'd find a soggy mess of a morsel breaking apart in the now rather dirty water. I can't blame the dry food in the water dish entirely on Lily, though. I think that sometimes Buttercup would intentionally do that in order to soften up some of the food before eating it.

Buttercup wasn't always able to clean up after Lily. Sometimes food that Lily dropped ended up underneath the dishes. The only time Lily would clean up the mess she'd made of dry food was in the morning while I washed their dishes. When I took the bowls to the sink to be washed, she would inspect the floor and clean up any pieces of food that remained. There was no way I could get the bowls cleaned, refilled, and returned to her fast enough. I think she figured that she'd starve if she didn't eat whatever she had previously tossed to the floor. By the time I got back over there with a wet rag to wash the floor, the food would be gone.

Buttercup not only cleaned up after Lily, but she'd clean up after me, too, especially when I used my George Foreman grill. If there's one truth on the Internet, it's that cats like cheeseburgers. Whenever I fired up that grill to make a cheeseburger, Buttercup would materialize in the kitchen within seconds. She was good about staying out of the way while I cooked and was smart enough to avoid the grill when it was hot, but after it cooled down, all bets were off. Once I realized that she would pull the grease-filled drip tray out from under the grill and lick it clean, I always put it up where she couldn't reach it. Or I would drop it into a sink full of soapy water. I figured all that grease and fat wasn't good for her, despite how tasty it must have been. I would leave the grill open to cool down before I cleaned it, but soon I realized I couldn't do that, either, otherwise she would lick it clean, too.

While Buttercup would politely eat from her bowls like a lady, Lily was a bit of a problem child. She decided it was more fun to chase her food. She'd pick a piece out of the bowl and drop it on the floor. After staring at it for a bit, she'd give it a whack and watch it slide across the linoleum floor, and immediately chase after it. She might whack and chase it several times, but eventually she would pick it up and eat it from her paw.

This aggressiveness with her food also applied to any treats that I fed Lily by hand. Once again, Buttercup was the complete opposite. Whenever I gave Buttercup a treat, such as a bit of meat from my plate or a kitty treat, she would always gingerly grasp it with her teeth, pull her mouth back slightly, and then gently shake her head to make sure that she had only the treat in her jaws and not any part of me. Lily, on the other hand, had absolutely no concern for the safety of human appendages when it came to getting food. In one fluid motion, she'd swoop down on the food with her tongue, chomp her jaws down on the tasty treat, and gulp down the food, only occasionally pausing to chew. A couple of times, I just about lost a finger.

Bubba's approach to treats was completely different. It took him quite a while to comprehend the idea of taking a treat from a human hand. When I gave treats to the cats, the girls would gladly take theirs, but when I put my hand out with a treat for Bubba, he would lower his head and push it under my extended hand. He must have thought those girls were crazy. *You're not supposed to eat from a human's hand. Human hands are for petting cats!* He would do this several times before I eventually just set the kitty treat down in front of him. Then he'd sniff it and finally eat it. It took several attempts before he would eat a treat from my hand. Years later, he would still push his head under my hand once or twice before accepting a snack.

Like most cats, Buttercup did not appreciate taking medicine. One time when she needed to take a portion of a pill twice a day, I decided to crush it and mix it with some mushy, smelly canned food. Since the cats normally ate dry food, having canned food was a treat. Even though only Buttercup needed the medication, you can't give wonderfully smelly food to just one cat. They all want it. After all, who would eat dry food when there's Fancy Feast? Sometimes slipping the crushed pill into this food would work, but other times it wouldn't. This activity did accomplish one thing: it trained me to feed them canned food twice a day. The cats became so accustomed to getting their tasty Fancy Feast that they would guilt me into giving it to them even when there was no medicine to be dispensed. On the plus side, since they were busy eating the smelly wet food, I was often able to clean the water and dry-food bowls without any assistance.

Buttercup was very polite and patient while I prepared the canned food. Well, for the most part. The cats would normally be on the floor staring up at me while their meals were being prepared. Bubba would sit off to the side near the table, Buttercup would be in the middle of the room, and Lily would be pacing back and forth at my feet, jabbering away and occasionally pawing at me since I was never fast enough for her. The tabbies were normally very quiet, while Lily wouldn't shut up until the food was going into her mouth. Buttercup would only occasionally speak. She would frequently jump up on the counter to supervise my progress, though.

As Buttercup aged, she seemed to want to supervise my actions even more. Due to arthritis, she was no longer able to jump up on the counter directly, but she could make her way there using a chair and the kitchen table. It seemed that every time I served canned food, she was right there on the counter watching me, and would often eat her meal there.

Eating on the counter also meant that Buttercup would get to start eating first, much to Lily's chagrin. This never bothered Bubba. In fact, after I put his plate down in front of him, he always looked over at the girls to make sure they were also eating before starting his own meal. If either one of them (normally Lily) decided that she wanted what was on his plate, he would politely back away and let her have it. That didn't happen often, but it was the only situation in which Bubba ever showed submissiveness to Lily.

It also trained me to stay in the kitchen and hover over Lily while she ate in order to keep her nose on her own plate. Occasionally she'd forget and I'd have to drag her back to her own serving. She'd complain to me about that, but she'd resume eating from her own plate. As soon as Bubba finished, I would no longer attempt to move Lily back to her own meal. Eventually, Lily figured that out and she learned not to attempt to eat Bubba's leftovers until he actually left.

Chapter 4: Quench a Thirst, Feline-Style

There is a mysterious phenomenon in California's Death Valley where rocks, some quite large, slide across the dry lake bed, leaving tracks in the sediment. To date, no one has ever witnessed these rocks moving. Several theories have been proposed, but not one of them has yet been proven. It seemed that a similar phenomenon was happening in my house. Occasionally, I would arrive in the kitchen to find that one or more of the cats' food-and-water-bowl sets had moved.

Even though I would arrange all of the stainless steel bowls neatly in a line against a wall, often one or more set would be pulled away from the others. Normally it was only a few inches, but occasionally they'd be moved several feet across the floor, sometimes clear to the middle of the kitchen. Like the sliding rocks of Death Valley, it was a mystery as to how the bowls moved, or at least, *who* was moving them.

In this case, though, someone was finally there to witness it. For a reason known only to her, Buttercup liked to tug at the legs of the base holding the bowls, often while she was drinking the water. She'd lap up some water, pull the bowls a bit, then lap up more water. I have no idea what she was trying to accomplish, but after moving the bowls, she seemed quite satisfied with herself.

It turned out that the floor wasn't the only place where Buttercup would pull water dishes. As she grew older, she liked to pull them from my hands as I was cleaning them. Each morning I would dutifully clean the water and food dishes, and while Bubba and Lily would patiently wait on the floor, Buttercup insisted on monitoring my progress more closely. She would stand on the counter to the left of the sink as I worked. Before I could even fill the water dishes with fresh water, she would grab at them, sometimes quite forcefully. As I filled each one, she would pull it close to her and start drinking from it. She had to drink the absolute freshest water, too. When she took a bowl away from me, I'd set it down for her and start to fill the next one. At that point, the first bowl was no longer good enough for her, so she'd yank the second one away from me. Sometimes she'd grab all three water bowls this way.

Seeing that happen, I decided to perform an experiment. Rather than setting a bowl down, I continued to hold it while she was drinking from it. I concluded that water must taste better if a human is holding the bowl because she would lap up as much as she could—more than she would if I just set the bowl down. Once she'd finally had her fill, I'd replenish the bowl and place it on the floor with the others.

Her morning water bowl antics sometimes delayed my trip to work. If it looked like that was going to be the case I would just set the bowl down on the kitchen counter wherever she was, even if it meant balancing the bowl on the narrow ledge in front of the sink. When I returned that afternoon, the bowl normally would be right where I left it, although a few times I found it in the sink. Amazingly, any bowls that were left on the kitchen counter never ended up on the floor, even when they had been placed precariously in front of the sink.

There was one additional water bowl in the house. It was on the sink in the hobby room. I put it there for Buttercup soon after she moved in, since she liked to spend time in that room with me. Unlike the kitchen bowls, she would drink from this one but not move it. Lily drank from that bowl, too, and like Buttercup, she left it where I had placed it. It wasn't until Bubba moved in that this bowl started to move. Occasionally I'd hear a crash along with the sound of sloshing water as the bowl was pushed into the basin. After rinsing the bowl, refilling it, and placing it back on the sink, Bubba would once again shove it into the sink, sometimes before I even had a chance to step away. It seemed that, for whatever reason, Bubba did not want the bowl on top of the sink, but rather *in* the sink. Eventually, I determined it was a lost cause and gave in. Since the only thing I ever used that sink for was filling the water dish, I decided simply to leave the dish in the sink. Once I did that, Bubba was happy and no longer attempted to move the bowl. Fortunately, the girls didn't seem to mind stepping into the sink to get a drink.

Dish antics aside, Buttercup was normally very polite and ladylike with her water. She normally wouldn't drink directly from the kitchen faucet; instead, she'd wait for me to dispense the water. That wasn't the case in the bathroom. Apparently, the bathroom sink had great-tasting water. I believe Bubba was the first to discover this. As I would get ready in the morning, Bubba would jump onto the bathroom sink and wait for me to turn the water on so he could have a fresh drink. He learned about this one winter day when I turned the hot water on and let it run for a bit to heat up. By the time I was ready to use it, he had his front paws near the drain and was lapping up the stream as it fell. Bubba trained me to turn the bathroom faucet on for him even when preheating water wasn't necessary. It seemed like any time I went into the bathroom, he'd leap onto the right side of the sink and wait for me to turn the water on. As I reached over to turn the water on for him, he would lovingly rub my hand with top of his head.

Soon Buttercup learned the joys of drinking from the bathroom sink, too. I joked that I needed to install "his-and-cats'" sinks in my bathroom, as both tabbies would be on the sink looking for a drink. Bubba was polite and very respectful of Buttercup. Even though Bubba was always the first to jump onto the sink and would assume his usual position to the right of the cold knob, he would back away from the faucet when Buttercup got up there and decided she wanted a drink. He would patiently wait for her to finish before going back for his own drink. Interestingly, Bubba always grabbed the water as it fell or, if the flow was slow, he'd go straight to the opening of the faucet. Buttercup, on the other hand, preferred to drink the water just before it was about to get away down the drain.

Another drain in the house also fascinated Buttercup —the drain in the floor of the unfinished basement. This drain had a couple of small plastic pipes leading to it for things like the air conditioner condenser and the whole-house humidifier. Soapy water from the nearby washing machine also occasionally bubbled up at that drain. With the three bowls in the kitchen plus the one in the hobby room, there was always plenty of fresh water available to Buttercup, but for some reason she frequently felt the need to check out whatever was in the drain down in the basement. It was something she would investigate every time she'd follow me to the basement. One of my tasks when I arrived home after work was to scoop the litter pans at the other side of the basement. She'd come along with me, made sure I did my job, and would then go find her watering hole into the unfinished room.

While doing laundry one day, I noticed a buildup of a slimy substance on the concrete surrounding the drain. Upon closer inspection, I saw tiny little bugs moving about. I had no idea what they were, but I figured that area was in need of a thorough cleaning. I scrubbed the area with some diluted bleach and rinsed it clear by pouring a couple of buckets of water near the opening, letting it all fall into the drain. For a few days after that, I kept the door to that room closed to keep Buttercup from drinking from the freshly bleached area. She seemed a bit annoyed that the door was closed, possibly because that was the room where new cats were quarantined before they moved into the house. Did she think that perhaps another feline roommate was coming? After enough time had elapsed, I opened the door, and once again, she was happy to have full access to her territory.

Buttercup seemed to derive a lot of satisfaction from drinking from anything other than her normal dishes. One of her favorite places to get a drink was from a pot or pan on top of the stove. After using a pot on the stove, I would often fill it partially with cold water to cool it down and make it easier to clean. Then I would place the pan back on the burner in order to keep a cat from stepping on the still-hot burner. If I had used a cookie sheet in the oven, I'd place it on the stove and pour cold water on it for the same reason. Before I had a chance to wash the dishes, Buttercup would normally make her way to the stove and check out any pot or pan that I had left there. I guess that to her this wasn't just a drink, but rather a drink flavored with human food. What could be better than that?

I learned early on that if I didn't want to get cat germs in my drinks, then I needed to keep a close watch on any cups that I used. Apparently, water tastes better when it comes from a cup from which a human drinks. Occasionally I would forgot and leave an uncovered glass on the table. Soon I would hear *slurp...slurp...slurp* as Buttercup helped herself to my drink. This was especially annoying when I had just filled the cup and set it down for only a few seconds. Eventually, I decided it was just easier to put a lid on my water cup and use a straw.

Sometimes she pestered me for a taste of my drink. When she did, I would often let her have the last bit from the cup. She couldn't reach the water without my help, though, so I would hold the cup at an angle where her tongue could lap it up. It was a bit of a balancing act to keep from spilling the water yet getting it close enough to the rim for her to reach.

Buttercup was very persistent when she wanted a drink. Even if there was only a little bit of water at the bottom of a cup—as little as a drop or two—she wanted it and would do whatever it took to get it. She would stare down into the cup while she brought a paw forward to the base of the cup in order to slide it around. If it was near the edge of a table or counter, she would push the cup until it fell to the floor. If not, she would reach up and pull the top of the cup down, spilling whatever contents remained. I always tried to empty all cups that I used but sometimes I would forget or figure there was so little left she wouldn't bother with it. Many times, though, I heard the sound of a plastic cup being pushed off the kitchen counter into the sink or on to the floor. If I went to check up on her, she'd just give me an annoyed look. *What? I wanted a drink.*

In this regard, Buttercup was much smarter than the cat that lived with my family when I was a kid. One time, he tried to get a drink from the bottom of a tall plastic cup. Rather than pull the cup over when he realized he couldn't reach the liquid, he poked his head farther and farther into the cup until he choked himself. At that point, reflexes took over and he jumped back and quickly raised his head, flipping the cup into the air and flinging its remaining contents all over the room. Then he stared at me in disbelief. *What are you laughing at?!*

It didn't matter where the water was, Buttercup would find it. One day while perusing my local hardware store, I found a small battery-powered water fountain in the clearance aisle. I had been looking for a fountain but couldn't find one that I liked that was also reasonably priced. Not knowing how the cats would react, I didn't want to put too much money into one. This one had three illuminated plastic pillars that looked like candles. The candles were on a base containing a variety of small, polished stones. The middle candle was taller than the ones on either side. A small fountain of water came out of the top of the middle candle and appeared to emulate a flame when illuminated with the built-in yellow lights. The water then ran off onto the side pillars before draining back into the base. When I got it home, I installed some batteries, filled it with water, and placed it on a table in the hobby room. All of the cats checked it out, but

Buttercup was completely mesmerized by it. She wanted to play with it and drink the water. Eventually I had to turn it off and put it up so she couldn't get to it.

A few weeks later, I put some fresh water in it and moved it to the coffee table in the living room. I ran it for a while and then turned it off when I left the room. I didn't think much of it until some time later when I was in the hobby room and heard a crash from the other end of the house. I went to investigate and found the fountain on the floor, resting on its side, while Buttercup stood next to it looking up at me. The rocks were strewn about everywhere, as was the water. She *knew* there was water in that thing and she was determined to get it. The expression on her face seemed to indicate that she knew she had done something she shouldn't have done but that somehow it was my fault. *What? I'm just getting a drink! It's not my fault you put the water in such a hard-to-reach place!*

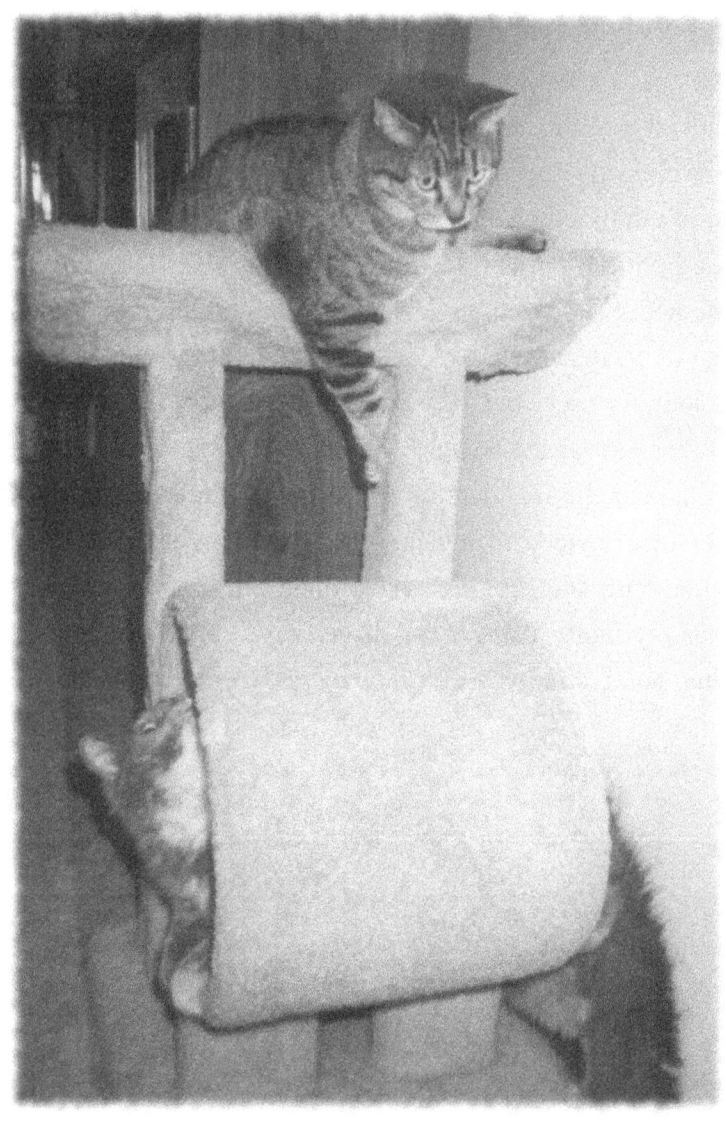

Queen of the Suburban Jungle

Chapter 5: Playtime

Like many cats, Buttercup was quite playful when she wanted to be. She liked to chase toys, particularly balls and mice. Although she could keep herself entertained, she loved the times that I would play along with her.

When Buttercup first moved in with me, she was still pretty young and energetic. She loved to chase toys all over the living room. She would hunker down wide-eyed, raise her butt, wiggle it back and forth, and then pounce on them or bat them across the room. I quickly discovered that she would easily get toys stuck in places she couldn't reach. If a ball or toy mouse ended up under the coffee table, she could frequently retrieve it, reaching in far enough to bat it out the other side. Only when it was clear in the center would she need my help.

The sofa was a completely different story. When she batted a toy under there, she would try hard to recover it herself, but usually it was too far away. She'd lower her head to look under the sofa and still try to reach for it. If she could get it out on her own, she'd continue to chase it; but if she couldn't reach it, she would start to cry, letting me know she needed help. When I heard her crying, I'd do my best to locate and extract the toy. Often I couldn't reach it with my paw either, but thanks to my opposable thumbs, I was able to grasp a yardstick to pull it out. Once the toy was within her reach again, she'd immediately start to bat it around.

Soon this became an all-too-frequent occurrence. Within seconds of freeing a toy, she'd once again have it stuck under the sofa and would be crying for me to help. I began to wonder if she was doing this on purpose just to have more interaction with me. Perhaps she was excited to learn that she could so easily manipulate me.

Regardless, something needed to be done. I purchased some boards and cut three pieces that would fit underneath the front and two sides of the sofa. The ends of the boards were beveled to align with the legs of the sofa. Instead of slipping under the sofa, the toys would now bounce off the boards, greatly reduced the number of stuck toys. She seemed to enjoy batting her pink Ping-Pong balls all over the place non-stop without fear of losing them. The boards stopped nearly all of the toys, but somehow, a few would still mysteriously slip past. She no longer informed me of them, though, so they would stay there until one of the very infrequent occasions when I'd pull the sofa away from the wall to vacuum the floor under it. Every time I did this, I was amazed to find a ball or mouse that had managed to make it by the barrier.

Buttercup had a variety of kitty toys. We would play together in the living room, where there was plenty of room to chase balls and throw mice around. At first, I kept Buttercup's toys in the living room while most of my toys were upstairs in the hobby room. Buttercup liked to be near me, so she spent a lot of time in my hobby room, too. She would get bored, though, while I was working on a project or typing on the computer. She was able to entertain herself with her own toys but wanted to be near me. What's a cat to do? She was a smart girl and knew how to solve that problem. She went to the living room, grasped one of her pink Ping-Pong balls with her mouth, and brought it up to my room. She dropped it on the floor and had a great time batting it around. When it got stuck somewhere, she would go get another one. Figuring that she could just barely fit one of those balls into her tiny mouth, I decided it would be much safer if I moved some of her toys upstairs for her so she wouldn't have to do it. She was appreciative of that and never again tried to move them herself.

If I was busy working when Buttercup was ready for playtime, she had a way of letting me know. Her method was to start playing with *my* toys. She would get up on the table and begin amusing herself with whatever small items she could find, such as pencils, pens, or small hand tools. To get my attention, she would push and slide these items around on the table. If that didn't work, she would select one to push off the table. After hearing that satisfying *slide...clunk* as the item went off the table and landed on the floor, she would turn and longingly look toward me. *Don't you understand it's playtime?*

Once I finally got the message, we would sit and play for quite some time, and she would leave my stuff alone until the next time. It's interesting to note that she only did this to get my attention. I could leave tools on the table at night or when I was at work and she would never touch them. It was only when I was in the room but not paying attention to her that she would mess with them.

There was one item that she liked to play with whenever I was using it: the tractor-feed strips from old computer paper. Before the days of ink-jet and laser printers, there were dot-matrix printers that used fan-fold paper. The paper was drawn into the printer using a tractor-feed mechanism with sprockets that grabbed holes along the sides of each sheet. These edges or "tractor-feed strips," as I call them, were meant to be torn off, leaving clean edges on the sheet. It turns out these tractor-feed strips provide nearly endless amusement for some cats. I discovered this one day after using an old printer. While removing the tractor feed strips, Buttercup became very interested in what I was doing and began reaching for the strips. We decided to turn this into a game since she loved to pounce on them, especially if I was also playing with them. While I sat on the floor, she would stretch out on the table and wait for me to poke the end of a strip up from underneath the table to where she could spot it and bat at it. Or, she'd wait for me to toss the entire strip on top of the table, where she'd take a swing and toss it back down to me. This would go on for quite some time.

If she was on the floor instead of the table, she'd chase the end of the strip as I dragged it along the carpet. She'd wait to attack until it was just about to disappear behind my foot or knee. Sometimes I placed the strip of paper under my leg, leaving one end visible, and then I'd slowly pull the other end. As the paper disappeared under my leg, she'd jump on it and, with both front paws, would attempt to burrow under my leg to get it. Sometimes she'd grab it with her teeth and pull it back. This game would get her very animated; she would start jumping around and making sounds. Often this game would climax with her getting so enthusiastic she'd exclaim, "*Mprrrrph*!" and then bolt out of the room.

Sometimes while playing the tractor-feed paper game, she wouldn't run out of the room but would instead run toward a newly installed bookcase. The third shelf from the bottom had an unused space about one foot wide. As she ran away from me saying, "*Mprrrrt!*" she would leap up to that open spot.

That spot wasn't just used for this game, either. She would sometimes make the short jump from the table to that shelf when we weren't playing any games, and would often stuff her head behind the books. I have no idea what was so interesting back there, but she always had to check it out. She was graceful and never knocked anything off the shelf, but I frequently had to push the first few books back in line with the rest once she was done.

One time I made the mistake of filling that spot on the bookcase with something other than a cat. Later, we were playing the paper game, and she headed for the bookcase. Somehow, she managed to stop, practically in mid-leap as only a cat can do, and look around in astonishment. *Where did my spot go?* After that, I did some rearranging in order to free up her place on the shelf. She continued to use that spot for the rest of her life. To this day, there is an open spot on the left side of the third shelf that is frequently occupied by a cat.

It turned out this shelf was also useful for games other than the paper game. She would stand up there and bat down mice and pom-poms that I tossed toward her. When she became fired up, she'd crouch down and wait wide-eyed for the next flying toy. We would do this until she grew tired of the game, but we'd be back at it the next night.

The paper thing wasn't her only table game. One of her playtime activities involved sitting or lying on the table while I sat on the floor and tossed pom-pom balls or little fuzzy mice up toward her. Her eyes would get big as she calculated the trajectory of each toy in preparation to bat it clear across the room, typically on the first swing. She was ambidextrous, too. I could often select which paw she used by changing the direction of my toss. I used to joke that she had "catlike" reflexes.

Playing with the tractor-feed paper strips would sometimes lead to another one of her amusing antics. After running out of the room, sometimes she'd run back into the room to chase the tractor-feed strip again, but other times she'd run all the way down the hall and leap off the end of the half-staircase on her way to the other end of the house. Where the staircase met the hallway, the gap between the balusters was a bit wider than the gaps between the other balusters. It was big enough that she could easily fit through it, even at full speed. It was one thing to see that little kitty butt flying through the air, but it was the sound associated with it that was priceless. You could hear the fast, periodic *patter-patter-patter* as she ran down the hallway before the sound paused briefly. It was then followed with a very loud *THUD!* as she hit the ground, but she never missed a step and that sound was immediately followed by *patter-patter-patter* that faded as she ran farther away.

Sometimes she would get worked up and make that running leap even when we weren't playing any paper games. No matter where I was in the house, I could tell where she was and what she was doing whenever I heard *patter-patter-patter-(pause)-THUD-patter-patter-patter.*

Tables, shelves, leaping from staircases—cats live in a vertical world. They love to climb trees and get in other high places where they can watch over their territory. Some cats don't like it when someone with a lower status is perched above them. Being in control of the house, Buttercup couldn't stand the thought of anyone mocking her, especially if that someone was a toy mouse. One time while we played with the balls and fuzzy mice, I balanced a mouse on the top edge of a folding chair. Her face took on a look of fury and determination. How dare a mouse sit up there and look down on her! She leaped up and whacked that mouse down so hard it flew halfway across the room. The higher the mouse, the more intently she attacked it. When she wasn't in the room, I would place a mouse at the corner of a table or on top of a chair. Later when she walked into the room and spotted the interloper, she would freeze with her stare fixated on it, quickly determine her plan of attack, and then dispatch that poor toy mouse.

When Buttercup played she would usually get quite excited, but there were times when she was subdued. While batting at a dangling toy, I would sometimes see her curl her paw slightly and pause while looking at the toy inquisitively as if attempting to understand the physics of the situation. She'd also do this while playing with a toy mouse on the table or floor. She'd take a whack, and then, with her paw still curled, she'd sit and stare at the mouse, possibly waiting to see what its next move would be.

Being a cat, Buttercup definitely had a mind of her own. There were times when she acted like she wanted to play but I think she really just wanted to test her control over me. I would drag a shoestring or tractor-feed strip across the floor but she would just look at it. I tried to remind her that it was a two-player game, but she would ignore me. She might not have been in the mood to play, but she enjoyed stopping me from what I was doing in order to give her attention.

When we played with the balls, pom-poms, or toy mice, Buttercup liked to bat at them or sometimes chase them. When she hit them, sometimes they would come back to me, but more often she whacked them across the room and expected me to retrieve them. It seemed I would get more exercise than she would when we played. Even when she chased them, she would never intentionally bring the toys back to me. After all, that was playing fetch, and fetch is a dog's game, not a cat's game.

Apparently, no one ever told Lily that. Lily also hadn't learned that games were to be played during the day and that nighttime was for sleeping, although I can't really blame her for that since cats are nocturnal creatures by nature.

When Lily was an adolescent, I awoke one morning around three to movement on the bed. Lily had jumped up next to me and had brought something with her. I was still half-asleep and trying to figure out what was going on. "What's this? A fuzzy ball? This shouldn't be here," I thought as I tossed the ball out the bedroom door and down the hallway. Before I could even put my arm back down Lily had bolted from the bed and was in the hallway, chasing her ball. I tried to go back asleep but seconds later Lily jumped back on the bed and dropped the ball at my hand, her tail eagerly flopping back and forth. "What the...?" I threw it again, and she once again took off like a greyhound chasing a rabbit. Moments later, she and the ball were back. "Oh, great, now it's a game."

Meanwhile, Buttercup rested at the foot of the bed, leaning against my right leg. She raised her head up briefly and looked toward Lily. *Why won't that kid just go to sleep, already?* At the time, I didn't know cats played fetch, but I now understand it's more common than most people think.

Shoelaces fascinated Buttercup. A cat's brain is wired to respond to the quick horizontal movement of a rodent. The back and forth movement of a dangling shoelace or string is reminiscent of that motion. As a young cat, she wanted to play with the laces as I tied my shoes. When one of my laces wore out, I replaced both of them and kept the old but intact lace as a cat toy. Buttercup enjoyed having her own shoelaces.

I would sit on the floor and pull her string along while she stalked it, pouncing just before it disappeared under my leg or foot. She would get quite excited by this, often grabbing my leg and kicking it with her hind paws. Other times, I would dangle the string in front of her or above her head and she would bat it back and forth. The only time I ever saw her sit up on her hind legs was to bat at a shoestring held over her head. As she grew older and more mature, she lost interest in most of the cat toys and left them for the youngsters, but she could never resist the temptation of playing with a shoelace that was quietly sneaking across the floor or table.

Buttercup's long hind paws reminded me of rabbit legs in both look and function. This was especially true when we played with string or paper and she'd get overly excited. Often she'd grab my leg with her front paws and start to kick with both hind paws simultaneously, practically bouncing off my leg while biting the shoelace or tractor-feed strip.

I could induce this rabbitlike characteristic by rubbing her belly, too. Some cats like to have their bellies rubbed, while others don't. My parents' cat Sparky liked to have his belly rubbed as long as it was his idea. He'd let you know when it was time—he'd lie down on his side, stretch out a bit, and expose his belly. Bubba would occasionally do that, too. Buttercup, on the other hand, didn't particularly care for belly rubs. She wouldn't complain but she would certainly start to kick, and if I didn't heed her warning, the amount of force she used quickly escalated. I learned not to push this too far because she had no qualms about using her claws.

Despite her fascination with shoestrings, she was normally very good about knowing which strings had been given to her as toys and which had not. Once she had her own shoestring toys, she never bothered with the laces on my shoes, even as they flopped around while I tied them. She also rarely grabbed at other strings or stringlike things, such as electrical cords. A couple of exceptions were the cords for the mini-blinds at the office and kitchen windows. I solved this by tucking the cords between the blinds as high as possible. This did not present an inconvenience, since I rarely adjusted either of those blinds.

As the other cats moved in, they discovered other stringy things that Buttercup completely ignored. Lily liked to rub against cords that were plugged into electrical outlets. Fortunately, she was smart enough not to bite one. She also occasionally pawed at wires on my workbench.

Bubba never bothered with electrical cords or wires, but found a different string that the girls completely overlooked. He managed to find another mini-blind cord that Buttercup, for whatever reason, always ignored. He discovered it one day when I opened the blinds on the casement window next to the workbench in the hobby room. I let the cord drop freely as I had always done, but the resulting pendulum motion was too much for him to resist. Fearing that he might become caught up in it, I learned to tuck the end of the cord between the blinds as high as I could. He would look at it but it was always just out of his reach.

Chapter 6: A Body at Rest

Cats spend a lot of time sleeping, typically sixteen to twenty hours a day. It makes sense—all of that eating and laziness is hard work and can wear a kitty out. Like most cats, Buttercup was an expert at napping.

Buttercup loved to be near me. While my lap was her favorite place to doze off, sometimes she preferred to sleep near me rather than on top of me. One of my computers was at a desk with multiple shelves. Atop the uppermost shelf was a flatbed document scanner. With a well-executed jump, she could make her way to that shelf and, more importantly, to the scanner. It was big enough for her to position herself comfortably for a nap. If the scanner had recently been used, it would be warm—an added bonus.

The scanner provided a high observation point, but it was rather exposed. Sometimes she preferred to find a cozier place for a nap. For the first few years, this computer had a bulky CRT monitor. When it was replaced with a thin LCD monitor, a new cat-hiding place opened up. Buttercup would slip past the side of the monitor and curl up behind it, under the shelf. Every so often, I'd have to clean out the fur that would collect in that semi-enclosed space. The fur also wreaked havoc on the computer's mouse. I had to clean the optical sensor daily, otherwise I'd have erratic mouse behavior.

To the left of the computer desk was a metal, four-drawer file cabinet. This cabinet was rather utilitarian and boring, containing papers, manuals, and various cables. But to a cat, it must have been incredibly exciting. The drawers were rarely opened, so when one was pulled out Buttercup insisted on checking it out. *Wow! A place I can't normally see or enter! Must investigate!*

The cabinet also provided a high vantage point from which she could keep an eye on things. On top of it was a small TV set. Once Buttercup made her way to the top shelf of the computer desk, it was an easy step to the top of the cabinet or TV. Like the flatbed scanner, there was a chance the TV would provide a warm napping spot, which was especially nice in the evening after the day's sunbeams had left.

Across the hobby room was my Linux computer. Whenever I worked at that computer, Buttercup loved to lie on top of the monitor, since it was not only warm but also close to me. For a long time I resisted replacing the old CRT with a more energy-efficient LCD monitor since I knew she would miss the warm shelf that the old monitor provided. I finally replaced the old tube display with a modern flat screen a month before Buttercup's passing. In that month, there were a couple of times when she got off my lap and walked around to the side of the monitor, as she did when she was going to go sleep on it. When she saw that there was nothing back there, she seemed disappointed. After that happened a couple of times, I slide the new LCD monitor forward and put the old monitor back in its place behind the new one, in case she wanted to lie on it.

To the right of the monitor was a portable radio and CD player that she would often walk on top of on the way to her heated nap space. Unfortunately for me, she wasn't too concerned about where she stepped as long as she was able to get where she needed to go. That's not good when something has a lot of buttons. She would frequently turn the radio off or on, change settings, or activate the "sleep" feature. Perhaps she didn't care for my taste in music? A few times I came home to find the door to the top-loading CD player opened, too. At least she was kind enough not to damage any CDs.

Buttercup had one other peculiar way of resting in the hobby room: on her back, with her paws in the air and belly exposed, and with her tail sticking straight out. This was a bit contrary to her normally proper and modest behavior. Usually she would perch in a very ladylike manner where she could keep an eye on things, especially if the youngsters needed to be supervised. But when they weren't in the room, she would sometimes get very relaxed. She'd lie on her side for a while, maybe playing with a ball or toy mouse, but when she tired of that and felt very at ease, she would roll over onto her back. All four paws would be up in the air, with her hind paws held close to her and her front paws folded back or stretched out. The tip of her tail would twitch endlessly as she lay there observing an upside-down world. This normally happened on the floor of the hobby room, but she was known to relax in that position on the living room floor, too. I've tried it, and yes, the world does look fascinating upside down.

While she seemed very relaxed in that position, she never let her guard down. If I approached her, she would normally roll back onto her side, probably to protect herself from a potential belly rub. If I brought a shoestring with me, though, she would play with it and even roll on her back from one side to the other while attacking the string.

Later in her life, Buttercup preferred my lap, but there was a time when she frequently would lie on my chest. For several weeks, we had a habit where I would lie down on the sofa under a blanket after work and supper to watch reruns of *The Simpsons*. During the show, typically near the end, Buttercup would decide it was cuddle time and would jump up on the sofa with me. She would lie down on her stomach, facing me, or on her side with her head near mine. I would softly stroke her silky fur, and if she was on her side and I put my arm around her, she would reach out and touch my upper arm with her paw. This affection was so enjoyable, especially while I was still developing a strong bond with her, that I never wanted to disturb this interaction. Instead, I always waited for her to decide to get up first. This was back in the days when I had very old TV with a rotary channel selector and no remote control. As such, I was subjected to whatever came on after *The Simpsons*. Back then, it was one of the *Star Trek* series. Despite not being a "trekkie," I ended up watching portions of several episodes while taking in this closeness with Buttercup.

As she became older, she wouldn't lie on my chest anymore, but would still occasionally join me on the sofa. If I stretched out on my side, she would lie on my thigh. She normally wouldn't do that if I had a blanket over me, but if she showed interest in cuddling, I'd push the blanket down and she'd jump onto my leg. This was never a discomfort, since she would keep my leg just as warm, if not warmer, than the blanket did.

Buttercup rarely sat or lay on the sofa without me. She would do it, though, just to keep me guessing, especially if there was something else on the cushions, such as a blanket or a worn sweatshirt. Normally, she hovered near me while I was getting ready for bed, but there were times when I was just about to check out for the night and realized I hadn't seen her in a while. I'd make a pass through the house, sometimes even turning the living room light on, and, of course, fail to spot her since I wasn't expecting to find her on the sofa. Only after I went back for a second, more thorough look, would I find her on the sofa looking up at me quizzically. *Are you looking for me?* After petting her and socializing with her a bit, I'd head off to bed. Invariably, I'd soon feel her jump onto the corner of the bed and lie down somewhere next to me.

There were times that she would sleep with me on the sofa, too. There was a period in my life when I suffered a reaction to an unknown allergen that often left me feeling sick to my stomach at night. When that happened it was difficult to sleep and uncomfortable to lie in my normal bed. Instead, I would sleep on the sofa where I could prop myself up with a pillow against the sofa's arm. Buttercup still slept on my bed, possibly figuring that I'd be back soon. Or maybe she just enjoyed the warm waterbed, since it was wintertime. After the first few nights of doing this, she figured out that something wasn't right and would check up on me. She wouldn't always sleep with me on the sofa, but on a good morning, I'd wake up to find that she had joined me during the night. If I had slept on my back, I would find her lying on my legs. When I slept with my back against the back of the sofa, I would find her lying on top of me, balancing on my side.

Buttercup loved being on my lap, but refused to sit or lie on my bare legs. She had no concerns about my bare hands or arms touching her, but she couldn't stand the thought of her paws being in direct contact with the skin on my legs. This wasn't an issue for most of the year, as I normally wore blue jeans. During the warmer months of late spring through early autumn, I would frequently wear shorts, always to Buttercup's dismay. When she jumped on to my lap, she tried to sit on whatever fabric she could find, but that wasn't very comfortable for either of us. I eventually decided to keep a hand towel near the table in the hobby room during those months. Whenever Buttercup decided it was time to sit on my lap, I'd spread the towel across my legs. If the towel weren't there, she would look at my lap longingly without jumping on it, but as soon as the towel was in position, she would be on top of it.

It was all psychological, though. If she didn't see that she was touching my legs, everything was fine. It was like the old *Roadrunner* cartoons where the coyote would run off a cliff but gravity wouldn't take effect until he looked down and saw that he was no longer on solid ground. Buttercup could be reclining happily on the towel on my lap, but then she'd move around a bit, either to stand up to be petted or just to reposition for more comfortable napping. During this repositioning, the towel might shift or even fall off my lap completely. If she didn't notice the towel had fallen away, she was fine. It wasn't until she looked down and saw that her paws were lying on my bare legs that she panicked. She'd jump down or at least stand and slide back toward my shorts to get her paws back on fabric.

I think part of her aversion to my bare legs was due to my reaction when we played together earlier in her life. Unlike Bubba and Lily, Buttercup had spring-loaded claws. They would pop out if she got frantic about anything or if she felt that her footing was uncertain. When we played with the tractor-feed strips or shoestrings, I'd often sit on the floor and pull them under my leg. She'd perk up and stalk the end of the string or paper, attacking it just as it disappeared between my leg and the floor. She'd get so fired up chasing the toy that she'd wrap her front paws around my leg and kick it with her hind paws. That was fine as long as I was wearing jeans. If I had shorts on, though, my reflex was to pull back with a yelp as soon as those claws hit my skin. After experiencing that a few times, she started avoiding my bare legs. I was never able to convince her that it was all right for her paws to touch my bare skin.

When Lily was unable to get to the fireplace mantle or the top of the entertainment center, I decided to add a tall cat tree to the living room to help her in her quest for vertical space. I built it using plywood, pieces of two-by-four lumber, sections of large cardboard tubes, and some carpet scraps obtained from a coworker. I thought it would be a nice winter project that would take a weekend or two. Instead, it took nearly two months of evenings and weekends. It was too cold to work in the unheated garage so despite the cramped conditions I built it in the basement.

In the end, I had a 127-pound beast that could barely fit up the staircase. It was sturdier and better constructed than the mass-produced models at the store. It had seven levels, two tubes, one enclosed condo with multiple viewing windows, and several open perches. The enclosed portions were completely carpeted, unlike the store versions. All of the carpet was glued and stapled, and in some locations, even sewn together. Normally, the carpet on commercially made cat trees is just stapled on. When the project was done, I realized I may have over-engineered it, but it certainly has withstood the test of time.

All of the cats enjoyed the cat tree at different times of their lives. For the first few years, Bubba decided the top perch was his. If he saw Lily up there, he'd scale the tree and kick her out, making her go down at least one level. Later he lightened up and decided it was OK if she slept at the top. Buttercup didn't spend a lot of time on the tree, but would explore it now and then. Not once did Bubba ever evict Buttercup from any spot on the cat tree, providing further evidence that Buttercup was in charge. In her later years, Buttercup liked to sleep in the short tube that was just below the top shelf. The smaller tube was the perfect size for her frame. When she took a nap in that tube, she liked to curl into a heart-shaped pose. She was the only person I knew who could sleep with her nose touching her feet.

Whenever I spent time in the living room, Buttercup frequently napped nearby. She had many places to choose from: the built-in bookshelves, two cat trees, the sofa, the mantle, the entertainment center, and several others. When she tired of her usual spots, she would look for some of her less-frequently used places. One of them was a small cavity created by the positioning of the wooden entertainment center next to the brick hearth of the fireplace. This space was just the right size for her to curl up out of sight. Interestingly enough, she never utilized a similar triangular spot on the opposite side of the fireplace, next to the cat tree.

The office contained an old flatbed plotter that was also one of Buttercup's more secret napping locations. Often when I couldn't find her on my first pass through the house, I'd spot her there on my second pass. She had been sleeping there for some time before I noticed. Normally there was a protective cloth cover over the plotting surface, but one day I noticed it had been disturbed a bit. I straightened it out, but a few days later, it was once again askew. I figured it had to be one of the cats—most likely Buttercup—but it was still several weeks before I actually saw her there.

One of Buttercup's most adorable mannerisms was crossing her paws in front of her when she lay down. In this very ladylike pose, she was beautiful and visibly confident, holding her head high, as she quietly surveyed her territory. She would lie with her front paws crossed on the coffee table, on the living room floor, on the kitchen table, in the hobby room, and at the plant window in the kitchen. She would also cross her paws when she relaxed in her sphinx-like pose on the mantle. She seemed to know that her ancestors in ancient Egypt were worshipped as goddesses. She allowed herself to be admired, but she never let it go to her head.

She was equally adorable in her single-paw pose. In that posture, she would lie down on her stomach with both hind paws and one front paw tucked underneath, while extending her remaining front paw in front of her. I noticed that Bubba would occasionally lie like that, too. Perhaps this is a common cat pose, or maybe he learned it from her.

Napping in the Plant Window

Chapter 7: Bedtime Stories

As I recall, Buttercup didn't share my bed right away when she moved in. I guess it makes sense. It was still early in our relationship so it was best to take things slowly. About a week or so after moving in, she started curling up next to me at night.

For the first two years, she wouldn't get on the bed unless I was there. During the day, she would take naps in any other part of the house but never on the bed. At night, she would wait for me to get in bed first. She would often sit and wait on the headboard while watching me get ready for bed. Sometimes she'd jump down right away, and other times she'd stay up there for a little bit longer before joining me. I always kept the left side of the headboard open for her, since that was the side that was easily accessible and the side she seemed to prefer. Occasionally she'd want to walk to the other side of the headboard but a reading pillow that I kept there usually blocked her path. If I saw that she wanted to walk over there, I'd set that pillow on the floor. Eventually I just moved it to a different location.

When it was time to join me, she'd jump down to the side of my regular pillow before deciding where she was going to lie down for the night. Despite jumping close to my head, she had excellent control and was very good about not landing on me, except once. I'm not sure if she slipped or just misjudged the leap in the dark. I heard her getting ready to make her move and the next thing I knew, she landed on my right temple, practically knocking me out. I've had worse things happen to me, but having an eight-pound cat land on your head hurts, although I think I was more surprised than anything. I was just glad she kept her claws retracted. She didn't seem fazed by her less-than-stellar landing. She proceeded to find a spot next to me and settle in for the evening as I drifted off to sleep, still dazed from the impact.

When Buttercup was younger, she would frequently remind me of bedtime. If I stayed up late for some reason, she would find me and attempt to get my attention, starting by simply entering the room and staring at me. She was patient, but cats know that humans are usually too dumb to understand what they are trying to say, so sometimes she got more aggressive.

Since I was frequently working at a computer, one of her common methods was to jump onto the table and walk across my keyboard two or three times. She'd then sit adjacent to the keyboard or perhaps in front of it, blocking my view of the screen. Sometimes she even sat on my right hand so I couldn't type or move the mouse. Sometimes she'd give up for a while and leave the room, only to return and stare at me even harder a few minutes later. *Why are you still up? Don't you know we're supposed to be cuddling in bed by now?* When I finally got the message and stopped what I was doing, she would jump down and follow me around until I made my way to the bedroom. She'd would then take her place on the headboard and wait for me.

Not only would she remind me of bedtime, she would also function as my alarm clock. Her method for this was to paw at the sheet and blankets and start to pull them away from me. *Hey! C'mon, it's time to get up! Time for breakfast!* If I didn't respond, she would pull them down even farther. If I still didn't respond, she would give up, only to try again several minutes later.

One morning she tried a new tactic for waking me. I think she had been watching too many of those cartoons where the antagonist lifts the eyelid of the protagonist when he is asleep, exposing a hilarious phrase spelled out in his pupil such as, "Out cold." Since Buttercup didn't have thumbs, she couldn't lift my eyelids, but she discovered that she could wake me by touching her wet nose to one of my closed eyelids. I'm thankful that she chose not to use that method very often.

I'm also thankful that she never taught that move to Lily. Unlike Lily, Buttercup was smart enough to know that I couldn't get out of bed if she was standing on top of me. That was a concept that Lily could never quite grasp. When Buttercup attempted to get me out of bed, she would stand next to me rather than on top of me. Lily would walk across me several times in the morning, letting me know it was time for breakfast. She'd then lie on top of me and continue to pester me about the lack of breakfast, yet when I tried to get up she wouldn't move. Sure, she wasn't really stopping me since I could have easily picked her up and moved her, but that just wasn't my style.

Buttercup normally wouldn't sit on me to wake me up, but sometimes she'd wake me up by chattering at the window. This normally happened in the spring and early summer, when she'd hear birds in the tree outside our bedroom window. The window was too far away from the bed for her to get a good look, but I'd open the blinds occasionally so she could at least sit on the bed and see what was happening on the other side of the window.

Even after living in my house for a couple of years, Buttercup would still not get on the bed without me. I thought that was odd, since human beds tend to be a favorite place for cats to sleep. Every indoor cat I've ever known has slept on a human bed. Apparently, no one ever taught Buttercup that it was acceptable to do that. Instead, she always politely waited for me. That was, until Lily moved in.

Lily was as active as a kitten could be, but she was also an expert at being lazy. As she got older, she sometimes ate lying down. Now that's a lazy cat. She also appreciated a good nap and wasn't afraid to just take what she wanted. The first time she jumped onto my bed without me, the panicked look on Buttercup's face was priceless. *What are you doing?! You can't be up there! There's no human! You have to wait for the human!*

Lily didn't care. Soon she taught Buttercup not to care, either.

Once Buttercup learned that it was acceptable to be on the bed without me, her nighttime routine changed slightly. If I stayed up too late, as I often did, she'd remind me about bedtime but eventually she'd give up on me and just go to bed herself. As I would get ready for bed, she might raise her head and look at me. *Oh, you've finally decided to join me?*

When it was just Lily and Buttercup sharing my house, I could still find a place on the bed. Once Bubba moved in and grew up, things started to get crazy. There would be times that I'd walk into the bedroom at night and turn the light on to find a bed with three cats strategically placed to maximize space utilization. Lily would be on the left side, Bubba would be somewhere on the right, and Buttercup would have chosen a spot in the middle. Where did they expect me to sleep? There was an empty corner—I guess they figured I would just curl up into a ball over there.

Bubba was always rather jittery, so often he would jump off the bed when it looked like I was getting ready to get in. Not Buttercup. *I tried to tell you. You should have gotten here earlier.*

If she was near the foot of the bed, it wasn't an issue. But there were times when she would pick the middle of the bed, and she seemed especially fond of the middle near my pillow. She'd be curled up with her back against my pillow and would barely acknowledge my presence. I would try to wedge my way in under the blankets on the side opposite Lily. About half the time, Buttercup would stand up, slowly stretch, and then walk to another part of the bed, surrendering her spot. The rest of the time, she stood her ground. Or more appropriately, *lay on* her ground. I tried to get as far under the blankets as I could, pressing my back against hers, but there were times when a leg or arm or even half my body was uncovered. But at least Buttercup was comfortable. By this point, it was becoming clearer who was in charge at my house. It was nice, though, having her close to me. I wouldn't have traded that for anything.

Lily liked to burrow under blankets on the sofa. She'd do that when I was there and when I wasn't, so I learned always to check the lumps on the sofa before sitting down. When Lily burrowed, I called her my "undercover kitty." Interestingly, she only did that on the sofa and not the bed. On the other hand, Bubba would crawl under the blankets on the bed, but only when he didn't feel well. When I saw a little white-and-brown nose sticking out from a lump of blankets, I knew it was time for a trip to the Cat Clinic.

Buttercup was never an undercover kitty. On the bed or on the sofa, she'd always sleep on top of the blankets. This didn't mean the explorer in her wouldn't occasionally take over. She'd act interested in the spaces that would open up if I lifted the sheet and blankets. Sometimes she'd just poke her head in for a look but lose interest right away; other times, she'd explore deep into the abyss. Slowly and methodically, she'd crawl alongside me before climbing over my legs to inspect the other side. Eventually she'd turn around completely and head out the same way she went in, and would then proceed to a spot on top of the blankets, tamping them down with her front paws before lying down and curling up next to me.

Buttercup's preferred spot on the bed varied greatly from week to week and changed over the years. When she first moved in, she would lie closer to my chest, but over time, she moved farther down the bed. One time while she was walking around next to me, I pulled the blankets down a bit. She decided to lie to the side of my chest as I lay on my back with my left arm mostly under the pillow. I discovered that if I tried to roll on to my side next to her, she'd get up and find another spot. So the next night, I just lay still. Again, she curled up next to me with her head touching my arm. It was very sweet the way she slept next to me like that, but she only used that spot for about a week before moving on.

Sometimes she would lie at the foot of the bed. Other times she would be somewhere along the side. I've heard of cats who lay on the pillow and wrapped themselves around their human's head, but that was the one place Buttercup never slept. She might walk across the pillow once or twice (or more) each night while looking for her spot, but she never stopped to lie on the pillow.

Her only requirement for selecting a place on the bed was that it needed to be somewhere she could touch me. If she were near the foot of the bed, she would lie next to or sometimes even on top of my feet. If she was farther up the bed and I was lying on my side with my legs bent, she would curl up between my legs and stomach. Or if she wanted to be behind me, she would settle in behind my knees on the hammock created by the blankets suspended between my hips and calves. Sometimes she would lean against my back. There were even a few times that she would lie on my legs. Regardless, she had to be touching me. If I moved during the night, she would adjust her position so that she was still touching me.

When Lily moved in but before Bubba joined us, Lily would also lie on the bed. The girls would lie on top of the blankets on either side of me, practically pinning me down. There were times when I woke up and wanted to roll over but felt cat weights both in front of and behind me. "Well, I guess I don't need to roll over right now," I would think before resigning myself to falling asleep in the same position. After Bubba moved in, he seemed to take over that role from Lily. From then on, it had to get pretty cold before it became a "three-cat night." Ironically, Lily would still lie on the bed with the two other cats if I wasn't there, but as soon as I got into bed, she'd jump down. Lily would still jump onto the bed when I was there, but typically only in the morning. Each morning I could tell how much food remained in their dishes by how annoying Lily would be. If she called me from the hallway and only jumped on the bed briefly, there was still enough leftover food. If she walked across me multiple times, talked to me constantly, and lay down on my chest, the dishes were empty.

Occasionally, Buttercup would lie on top of me in bed. This normally involved my legs or hips, but more than once I found her balanced on my side. One morning we both awoke a bit earlier than normal. I turned over to lie on my back and went back to sleep. I recall her climbing onto my chest, but forgot all about it as I drifted back to sleep. The next time I opened my eyes, it was a bit of a shock to find myself face to face with a cat. I think I was so startled that I jumped a bit and then started to laugh, but Buttercup, in her naturally calm way, wasn't bothered by my response.

Buttercup was very trusting of me in bed. If she was lying between my calves and I wanted to roll over, I could do so under the blankets and she wouldn't leave or complain. As soon as I was settled, she would make any adjustments necessary in order to be touching me again, and would then go back to sleep. There were also times when I would roll halfway over from my side to my back.

Without moving herself, she would start that journey on my legs and end up between them, or if she had been on my pelvis, she would end up on my stomach.

Normally, Buttercup would get out of bed in the morning whenever I did. Her morning ritual was similar to mine: she'd stand up, stretch a bit, jump down from the bed, and perhaps stretch a bit more, sticking her hind legs out behind her one at a time. OK, I don't do the leg thing. As she grew older and wiser, she decided that perhaps sleeping in was a better way to respond to the morning. She would always wake up with me and nearly always come for breakfast, but rather than getting up right away, she'd lie on the warm bed and keep an eye on me and the other cats while we went through our morning routines. Eventually, she would stand up to arch her back and then jump down to do her stretching before casually making her way to the kitchen. She might not show up while I washed the water and dry-food dishes, but normally by the time I served the canned food, I would turn around to find her looking at me.

There were a few days that she stayed in bed even while I prepared the canned food. Typically, these were winter days when the house was cool and the desire to enjoy the heated waterbed outweighed the need for smelly, mushy food. The first few times this happened, I had already prepared her food and was surprised when she didn't show up for breakfast. Since it was odd for her to miss breakfast, I went to check on her and took the food with me. She was fine, so I presented the food to her.

Soon, I realized that I was serving breakfast in bed to a cat. How did this happen? She only received that treatment a few times before I decided not to prepare her canned food unless she showed up in the kitchen with the other cats.

Later, Bubba would also try staying on the bed in the morning, but by then I had learned that trick. He never managed to get breakfast in bed.

When I was a teenager, my family had a large, black tomcat. Every night, he would sleep on my bed in the same spot. He was there when I went to sleep and was there when I woke up. For years, he would spend the whole night with me, or so I thought. It turned out he had pulled an elaborate ruse on me for years. He waited for me to go to sleep, and then got up for a late evening or early morning prowl. Cats are, after all, nocturnal creatures. I discovered his method when I had trouble sleeping one night. I noticed that he got up, left the room, and went downstairs. The bed felt strange without a cat lying in the corner by my feet—even though he'd most likely gotten up every night for months, if not years.

I discovered further evidence of his tactics one morning when I awoke early and found him gone. About half an hour before my alarm sounded, he quietly made his way back upstairs and returned to his spot on the bed, thinking I was none the wiser.

Buttercup didn't do that. If I woke up in the middle of the night, I could feel her warmth next to me or on me. She would spend the whole night with me. Well, almost. I discovered one day that she had a habit of going on a brief early morning prowl. Based on my observations the few other times that I awoke early, I concluded that she prowled on a somewhat frequent basis. The preferred start time for her routine was between 5:00 and 5:30 a.m. She would quietly hop off the bed and leave the room to make the rounds of her territory, and perhaps stop by a litter pan. Like that black tomcat, she always returned to my bed about half an hour before my normal wake-up time.

When Buttercup first moved in, there was no problem about me tossing my pajamas on the bed in the morning as I got dressed for the day. Since she wouldn't get on to the bed without me, I never had a problem getting my pajamas back in the evening. After Lily moved in and both of the girls started to get on the bed without me, this didn't work out so well. Lily would leave my clothing alone but Buttercup had a desire to lie on any article of clothing that I left on the bed. I used this to my advantage while the cats were boarded at the Cat Clinic when I was out of town. Having familiar scents on unwashed clothing would help comfort them while I was away. At home, though, this presented a bit of a problem when I was ready to go to bed and found that my pajamas were already in use. Sure, I could pick the cat up and move her, but she looked so comfortable that I didn't want to disturb her. Occasionally she would only have part of her body on my pajamas and I'd been able to pull them out from under her without upsetting her too much by using the old yank-the-tablecloth trick. But I figured a better solution was to avoid the problem altogether. I never considered folding my pajamas and placing them in a drawer each morning or hanging them in the closet. Sure, that might have made my mom proud, but she wasn't around to witness it. Besides, that really was not my style. After all, I'd be using them again in about sixteen hours, so I was saving time. As a result, Buttercup trained me to put my pajamas under the sheets in the morning. Even if she lay on that part of the bed (and she often would), I could easily slide them out from under her since she wasn't in direct contact with them.

I discovered quite by accident that there was a wonderful benefit of doing that. The bed was a waterbed, so from mid autumn to mid spring it was heated. Pajamas set on top of the blankets don't absorb much heat (unless they have a cat lying on them). Pajamas *between* the mattress and the blankets absorb plenty of heat. It was like putting them on after taking them straight out of the drier! I thought, "Hmm... if it heats up pajamas, then perhaps..." Wow! It was great on a cold winter morning to get out of bed and jump into a warm shirt and toasty pants. At night, I kept my house a bit cooler than normal, but with a warm waterbed, the cool nights were never an issue. The mornings were a bit chilly at times, but after Buttercup trained me to put the next day's clothes under the blankets, that was no longer an issue. Thanks, Buttercup! In order not to rob her of the experience of sleeping on my dirty laundry when the season turned, I frequently left a worn shirt on her favorite corner of the bed. When there was no clothing on the bed, she would lie anywhere except the pillow, but if I put some clothing on the corner of the bed, she was irresistibly drawn to it.

Typically, I used Buttercup's favorite corner of the bed as my clothing warmer because it was the most convenient. This created a slight bulge, raising the bedding slightly. On those cold winter mornings when I'd slide my pants out from underneath the blanket she was lying on, she'd give me a disappointed look as I took this bulge away. *Hey, I was laying on those!*

Whenever she decided to join me in bed or on the sofa, Buttercup was always good about waiting for me to get settled. Only after I was comfortable would she jump up and find a place to curl up next to or on top of me. She set a wonderful example that Bubba was able to learn, but Lily was never able to pick up this habit. Every night, Bubba would curl up next to me on the bed, but only after I was in position. While I was getting comfortable, he would sit on the floor next to the bed and patiently wait for me. Nearly half the time that Lily decided to join me on the sofa, I was nowhere near ready, which only caused delays in both of us getting comfortable. Lily is a wonderful kitty, but she's quite impatient.

Lily's impatience was also evident when she walked to the kitchen with me. Whenever I went to the kitchen, Lily was not far behind, and if it were close to breakfast or dinnertime, she stayed so close to me that she would often trip me. She would be so eager for her food that she wanted to run ahead of me, but simultaneously she wanted to be behind me to make sure I didn't get lost on my way to the kitchen. I wonder if she ever became frustrated with how difficult it was to herd humans. As I started to walk, she'd run alongside me, and then cross in front of me and slow down. She'd go right, so I'd have to slow down and go left. Then she'd do it again but go left so I'd have to go right. All the while, she would be talking to me, complaining that I wasn't going fast enough. Buttercup was much more polite and would follow a comfortable and safe distance behind me. I don't recall a time when she ever got in the way. Perhaps Buttercup was also smarter, and knew that nothing good could come from tripping a human.

Part of the problem with following Lily to the kitchen was that, unlike a lot of cats, Lily tended to take the shortest path to her destination. It was a left turn from the hallway to the staircase, so Lily would cut the corner to the left, typically crossing directly in front of me. At the bottom of the steps she needed to make a right turn, so she'd move across the stairs in order to make the sharp right turn, once again crossing my path.

Buttercup used the more common feline philosophy of never taking the most direct route *anywhere*. Upon entering the bedroom, she'd walk beside the entire length of the bed before hopping up near the pillow or onto the headboard, only to proceed to a spot near my stomach or feet. Walking through a hallway often involved ducking into each doorway, if only briefly. The path from the hobby room table to the top of the toolbox could have been one simple jump, but instead consisted of a pass in front of a computer monitor (especially if I was using it), then a step on to the radio, then on to the monitor before finally reaching the toolbox. It might appear that she didn't know where she was going, but she always proceeded with confidence and a look of determination.

I recall Marty telling me she would get "walked on" a lot. I don't remember if she was referring to Buttercup or to another cat, but it certainly could have been Buttercup. When I sat on the sofa, it seemed that no matter where she wanted to go, Buttercup's path had to involve crossing my lap at least once. In the hobby room, too, if my lap wasn't her destination it was at least on her route.

I've always said that cats, as a rule, have little concern for human discomfort. I experienced this when Bubba used my stomach as a springboard to jump off the bed, or leapt out of my arms when he needed to escape from the room quickly, as cats tend to do. Lily wouldn't do that, but she would frequently walk across me. Often she'd stop and stand on me, using her front paws to focus a lot of her weight on a very small area. I had to be careful when she was near my neck for fear that she might choke me. Soon it became a reflex to cover my neck with a hand when I was lying down and Lily walked by. I never had these problems with Buttercup. When she got on the bed, Buttercup was always very good about lying down next to me in a way that was comfortable for both of us. She might walk across me, but she knew where she could put her weight without hurting me as she made her way to her chosen spot.

Opportunistic Water

Chapter 8: Behavior

Living with a cat for nearly fourteen years, one becomes accustomed to her mannerisms. It was interesting to observe her behavior in different situations and with different people, and how those behaviors changed over time.

Buttercup was a very sweet and understanding cat, but she did have a subtle way of letting people know I belonged to her. Or perhaps it was not so subtle. Back when she lived with the Mathers, Buttercup interacted with visitors on a frequent basis. When she moved in with me, she became more of a one-person cat.

Although she was always quite interactive with me, Buttercup was typically not social very with my guests. Whenever I had a visitor at the house, Buttercup would come out if for no other reason than to inform the guest(s) about the rules of the house, and rule number one was that

Jerome belonged to Buttercup. If a visitor were sitting in the hobby room with me, she would always jump onto my lap. If I was on the sofa with a date, she would do the same but with a twist. Rather than come straight to me, she would first strut past but otherwise completely ignore the visiting female. Then she would jump onto my lap and sit with her back to my date. The human female would take notice.

"Wow, she's pretty possessive of you."

I'd respond, "Don't worry, it's not you. She's like this anytime I have a guest."

At least when Buttercup chose to ignore someone, she did it with purpose and confidence. This was in contrast to a cat I knew at the shelter where I volunteered. That cat would turn her back to me to ignore me, but would then look back to make sure that I saw that she was ignoring me. Was this some kind of feline mind game? Buttercup never had that problem. If she chose to ignore someone, then as far as she was concerned, that person just plain didn't exist, and she didn't care one bit what that person thought.

Buttercup wasn't just demanding of my lap when there was a visitor in the house. She spent a good portion of her life warming my lap. The day I picked her up, Marty warned me, "I hope you like to sit because she's a lap cat." Those words were true to her last day. She would often spend an hour or more at a time on my lap. Depending on how I was positioned, I would often end up with sore body parts, particularly my legs, but also my feet if I had them up. As I've said, human discomfort is of no concern to cats. But she was happy, comfortable, and looked so peaceful. How could I disturb her?

As I stroked her back or gave her a chin rub, she would start to make her "happy sounds." Buttercup's happy sounds were a combination of a loud, long sigh and a purr. The sounds were often quite funny and would sometimes make me or anyone nearby laugh. My mom even commented one time, "Wow, she certainly is content!" When Buttercup made her happy sounds, I could feel the tension in her body melt away as she relaxed. This contentment was contagious—I never felt so at peace as I did when Buttercup was napping on my lap.

If I hadn't sat in a while, Buttercup would let me know that it was lap time. Normally this would happen in the hobby room, where she would walk along the tabletops close to me and start pawing at me. That was the sign that it was time for me to sit down. Naturally, I would obey. When I realized I was sitting at her command, it became clear to me that I was no longer the one in control of the household.

If it was lap time but I was busily moving about the house taking care of non-cat things, Buttercup had a way of letting me know. She would give me a certain look as she followed me around the house. As I made my way to a chair, she would follow me with purpose and immediately take her place on my lap when I sat down.

She would also sit at the edge of the computer desk near the doorway of the hobby room and look into the hallway. Her tail would hang off the table with its tip predictably twitching back and forth. Each time I walked by, she made sure I saw her until I gave in and sat down at the computer, at which point she would turn around and make her way to my lap.

She would also sit in this area if she decided I was paying too much attention to the computer and not enough attention to the cat. She would walk back and forth in front of me, sometimes walking or sitting on the keyboard, or on the cord to the mouse. There were times when I'd have to put the keyboard up to prevent her from causing problems with the computer. As soon as I gave her my lap and an appropriate amount of attention, all was well.

These behaviors showed that despite the fact that humans and felines speak different languages, we seem to be able to communicate fairly well. When Buttercup settled on my lap, she'd often face away from me while I softly stroked her back. Before she dozed off, she'd turn her head to the left and look back at me while purring softly. We'd look into each other's eyes and seemed to communicate our feelings perfectly. She'd turn back and let out a contented sigh before drifting off to sleep.

Not all of our communication was unspoken. Buttercup understood at least one English word: "no." She was very well behaved, so I didn't have to say it often, but then again, she was a cat, and cats tend to be rather curious, especially if something tasty is involved. While I prepared food, she liked to get onto the counter to check things out. As she approached something that I didn't want her to get into, I could tell her "no" and she would politely back away from it, never taking her eyes off it until she turned around.

When I told Buttercup "no," she listened. I don't recall ever having to tell her twice. On the other hand, Lily, the chowhound, had different ideas. She didn't get onto the counter very often, probably because it was normally too much effort for very little reward. But when enchanting smells were coming from the kitchen, she would find her way up there. I think she knew what "no" meant but chose to ignore it. She might stop briefly, but within seconds, she'd once again be moving toward the food. I would inevitably have to pick her up and place her on the floor, and she would always tell me just how she felt about that. In less than a minute, she'd be right back up there, hoping I'd forgotten. When I placed her on the ground again she would complain, huffing in frustration. In contrast, if I ever had to remove Buttercup from a counter and place her on the floor, she would just give a quiet *"mew"* of protest but then respect my wishes.

It's a common misconception that cats avoid or don't like water. Cats are actually drawn to water and would prefer to drink from a flowing stream than from standing water. Buttercup was especially fond of water wherever she could find it. Apparently, opportunistic water always tasted better than the fresh water I'd put out for her. When

I took a shower, I liked to let the water run for a moment to warm up. That can be problematic in a house where a cat is always looking for a drink from a running faucet. She'd hop right into the tub. Normally when I got into the shower, she wouldn't stick around very long. But one day she refused to leave. I finally turned the knob to redirect the water from the tub faucet to the showerhead. I did my best to keep Buttercup from getting wet. I pointed the showerhead down as far as it would go and attempted to block most of the spray with my body. After a bit, she decided that she was done and hopped around the shower curtain, leaving on her own terms.

I was quite surprised the day she decided to join me in the shower when I was already well into washing my hair. While lathering up, I felt something brush against my right leg. I looked down to find that Buttercup had gone around the shower curtain and was standing in the tub with me. I once again did my best to shield her from the water but this time she didn't seem concerned about it at all. She made her way toward the drain for a drink. She showered with me for two or three minutes before hopping out. When she got out, she stayed in the bathroom and waited for me. I finished up as quickly as I could and dried myself off. That's when I discovered that despite my attempts to shield her from the water, I had one very wet cat. She didn't seem to mind, and was very patient with me as I procured a clean hand towel from the linen closet and dried her off.

🐾 🐾 🐾

It's been said that inside every domestic house cat is the soul of a large wild cat. While this may not always be the case, it was certainly true with Buttercup. I could look into her eyes and become overwhelmed by her intelligence and free spirit. Buttercup was as stealthy as a lioness on the prowl.

I don't know how she did it, but she could slip into any closet I opened without me knowing, even if the door was only open for a few seconds. During the first year she lived with me, she ended up trapped in every closet and half the cupboards in the house. After hearing that muffled *"mrrrow!"* a few times, she had me trained to check for cats before closing any door I opened, even if it had been opened only briefly. When she decided some exploring needed to be performed, I'd often just leave the door open and go back to close it later.

Her quiet personality and small size gave her the uncanny ability to hide practically anywhere. Every day when I arrived home from work, I would check up on the cats. Often, they would greet me at the door. When Buttercup was the only cat, she greeted me at the door every evening. When Lily arrived, Buttercup contracted that job out to her. Lily would wait by the door for me, frequently meowing at me before I could even unlock and open the door, while Buttercup would sit at the top of the staircase looking down at us. Things became a bit more interesting after Bubba moved in. For some reason, when

I arrived home, he would tear down the staircase in a black-and-white blur, all the way to the unfinished portion of the basement, where he would stand underneath the staircase.

Cats are creatures of habit, so I was generally able to predict what I would see before I opened the door. But if any of this didn't happen, I would seek out any missing cats. When that missing cat was Buttercup, it was especially challenging. In order to find her, I would make several passes through the house, methodically scanning each room. The first pass would be fast, as I would check all of her usual locations. If I didn't spot her, I would make a second round to check the less likely locations. Sometimes I found her, but other times I couldn't, and that's when I would start to worry. Did she manage to sneak out somehow? Did she get too curious and become trapped somewhere? My heart would start to race as I began the third pass through the house, at which point she would nonchalantly meet me walking down the hallway. *Oh, were you looking for me? Here I am. What's for dinner?*

Some of the less common places I'd find her included on the middle shelf of a storage unit in the basement, behind the furnace, behind books on the built-in bookcase in the living room, in an open closet, and on top of a bookcase where she only had about six inches of clearance to the ceiling. I sometimes wonder if she just completely disappeared into another dimension, only to come back when she realized I was going to go crazy if I couldn't find her.

I think cats have the ability to warp the space-time continuum to their own personal liking. I personally witnessed this happen with Lily once. There was a small box on the floor that I had recently emptied. Like many cats, both Buttercup and Lily enjoyed new boxes, but Lily was more likely to get into them. This one was too small for her to sit in, though, and I informed her of that. "Lily, you can't fit in there," I told her. She proved me wrong as she wedged herself into the box, and then looked up at me with a smug expression. "What the…how did you do that?" Humans attempt to change their world, but in the feline world, the universe quietly adapts to suit the cat.

Buttercup was the only cat (so far) who explored behind the refrigerator. I don't know how she was able to fit back there, let alone make the turns around the corners, all the while traversing the slalom of the power cord and water line for the ice maker. She didn't go back there very often but sometimes when she became enthusiastic and ran through the house, she'd finish her run with a trip behind the refrigerator. For some reason, she'd always enter on the right side and almost always leave on the left. A few times, she would turn around behind the unit and come out the same way she went in. How was that even possible?

Buttercup loved to explore every nook and cranny of the house. It seemed that regardless of how many times she'd been to a particular spot, she always wanted to see it again. One place in particular was the coffee table. The table had two doors on one side that enclosed a large storage area underneath the table. Any time I opened one of those doors, she was right there, ready to jump in. It soon became even worse. The doors had handles that made a very distinct sound. She could pick up that sound from across the house. Any time I even bumped one of the handles, she would instantly show up, thinking I was opening the doors to her hidden space. In her later years, she was so interested in that compartment that she would often try to grab the handles herself, at which point I would comply and open the door. Soon I just decided to leave one of the doors unlatched so she could open it whenever she felt the need. The desire to explore that area seemed to be a trait unique to Buttercup, as I don't recall any of the other cats ever getting in there. They would occasionally poke their heads in when she was in there, but they would never enter.

Before moving in with me, Buttercup had spent a year or so living with the Mathers. One of the jobs she had was to escort the Mathers' granddaughter to or from school. On these trips, Buttercup would lie in the rear window of Marty's car and enjoy the view. This made her very accustomed to traveling in a car. Thanks to that, I had no trouble loading her into a pet carrier, even for trips to the vet.

The same could not be said for of the other cats. Bubba got by but didn't seem to enjoy traveling, and Lily was a nightmare; she absolutely did not want to leave the security of her house. She would put up a fight going into the carrier, and would start crying almost immediately. The crying wouldn't stop until we were seated in the waiting room. Buttercup was the complete opposite. I used to joke that I had to hide my car keys; otherwise, Buttercup might decide to go for a road trip on her own.

Buttercup was so good—in fact, eager—about traveling that it sometimes complicated things when it was time for a different cat to go to the Cat Clinic for a checkup. Sometimes I would need to get two carriers out because Buttercup would eagerly pry her way into the first one before I could load the correct cat into it. Once I wrangled the other cat into the second carrier, Buttercup would have a disappointed expression on her face, knowing that she wasn't going to go for a ride that day. When it was her turn to go, it made the trip very enjoyable knowing that she was happy.

Buttercup also received some special treatment when we left the house. Sometimes I'd place a box on the seat underneath her carrier so she'd have a clearer view out the window since she enjoyed the ever-changing scenery. In addition, she traveled so well that I didn't feel the need to take her directly home after visiting the Cat Clinic. We occasionally picked up dinner at the drive-through window of a fast-food restaurant. Buttercup seemed to enjoy these extra adventures.

Inspecting New Staircase

Chapter 9: The Problem-Solving Kitty

Like humans, different cats have various levels of intelligence and reasoning skill. Buttercup was one of the most intelligent cats I've ever known. While volunteering at Purrfect Pets animal rescue, I met a cat whose previous human described him as "a problem-solver kitty." That term was applicable to Buttercup, too. It was interesting to observe her approach to a situation compared to those of the other cats.

Take the bathroom door as an example. If Bubba was in the bathroom and the door was closed but not latched, he could get out, but only by accident. He'd lie down on the floor and fumble with the door, and eventually he'd get it to open. It took several years before he became proficient at opening the door and able to do it without lying down. Lily had a better understanding of door technology. Placed in the same situation, she could quickly open the door at will.

Buttercup, however, did better than either of them did. Not only could she easily grab the edge of the door and push it open, but if the door was latched, she would jump onto the sink and paw at the knob. She *knew* that the knob had something to do with opening the door. It appeared as though she was trying to get the knob to turn but couldn't make it happen. I can't imagine what she would have accomplished if she had had thumbs.

Another example of her intelligence and cognitive skills surfaced when I replaced the entertainment center. The old cabinet was short enough that she could get to the top in a single bound. From there, she could easily walk to the mantle, since the entertainment center was just to the right of the fireplace. The new unit was a bit taller. When it was first installed, no cat was able to reach the summit for several days.

Then one evening I saw Buttercup sitting in front of the new cabinet, staring at it intently. The look on her face spoke volumes; I could see the cogs turning in her mind. After studying the new entertainment center for about five minutes, she stood up and walked with purpose over to the fireplace. She jumped up onto the brick fire hearth, which got her about fourteen inches higher. That was all she needed: from there it was still a long jump to the top, but it was manageable. With her need to explore every nook and cranny, she jumped over to the mantle, explored its entire length, and then returned to the top of the entertainment center to curl up for a nap with a satisfied look on her face.

A few minutes later, Bubba walked into the room. When he saw her lying up there so proudly, he instantly froze and stared at her. *If she can get up there, I can too!* He ran to the edge of the entertainment center opposite the fireplace and looked straight up at it. Then he took a couple of steps back and his powerful hind legs propelled him to the top in one well-executed leap. Brute force was Bubba's primary tool.

Several days later, Buttercup was once again resting on her high perch overlooking the rest of us when Lily strolled into the room and saw her. Upset that Buttercup was up there, she began to whimper a bit as she hurriedly walked around the room, searching for a way up. This was going to be a difficult jump for Lily because she was a bit plump at the time and not nearly as muscular as Bubba. Picking up Bubba was comparable to picking up a cat-shaped cinder block—he was *all* Bubba—whereas picking up Lily was like trying to grab a water balloon.

Lily looked at the same side of the entertainment center that Bubba had targeted, but it was way too high for her. She walked across the room and jumped atop the small cat tree by the window. That got her halfway up, but then she was too far away from the entertainment center. She walked back to the front of the unit and paced for a while, occasionally looking up at Buttercup. She stood up on her hind legs but couldn't reach the top. After a while, she just decided to go for it and sprang up with all her might.

Her front paws didn't even reach the top shelf. Gravity wasn't on her side; she slid down in front of the TV with all four paws spread out cartoon-style. She landed safely, perhaps with her pride slightly damaged. Bless her little feline heart for trying.

Soon after Lily's failed attempt to reach the new high spot in the living room, I built a multilevel cat tree where the distance from any level to the next was no more than sixteen inches, well within Lily's capabilities. I positioned it to the left of the fireplace so that even Lily could easily work her way to the top and get to the mantle. In her later years, Buttercup also appreciated having easier access to the mantle and entertainment center.

Like accessing the entertainment center, laser pointers were another item that each cat responded to differently. Bubba went absolutely berserk with the laser pointer. Once again, brute force was his method. I've never seen him as animated as he was when he was chasing his red dot into the closet, out of the closet, across the floor, up the wall, onto the ceiling. *How did it get up there?* He would be practically panting from all the running he did trying to capture his dot. Lily also enjoyed playing with the red dot, but she was more amused than excited. She might paw at it and even chase it a bit, but she'd step aside as soon as Bubba heard the commotion and ran into the room. Buttercup, on the other hand, would occasionally paw at the dot, but otherwise she would look at me. She *knew* I was behind it, but she just couldn't figure out how I was making it happen. When Bubba was playing with the dot, she would just sit back and give me a stern look. *You might be fooling him, but you're not fooling me!*

There was only one activity at which I could fool her; I discovered it accidentally one day when we were playing the game in which I tossed toys into the air as she sat on the table and batted them down. As I went to toss a mouse, I inadvertently caught the tail between my fingers so it ended up not leaving my hand. She didn't see this, though, and looked up. *Where'd it go? I don't see it!* I tried it again, this time on purpose, and got the same response. Even if I made a quick upward motion with an empty hand, she'd fall for it. Her head would dart up and she'd look all over for it every time. *Where is it?! I'm an expert at this! How could I miss it?!* It made her even more determined to whack the next one that I tossed. Her pupils would dilate as she hunched down and prepared for her attack on the next mouse or ball.

Buttercup always had a very sweet disposition. Not only was she nice to me, she was also patient with and kind to the other cats that came to live in her house. She was also polite, if somewhat standoffish or indifferent, to visitors. She was even amiable when visiting the doctors and staff at the Cat Clinic. During the last six months of her life, she began suffering from kidney failure, so she went to the Cat Clinic three days a week for intravenous fluids. She was required to lie still for a few minutes while she was "topped off." All of the veterinary technicians raved about what a pleasure it was to give Buttercup her fluids because she was always so well behaved and ladylike. She never made things difficult for them and barely ever said a word. Once the fluids were done, she would stand up, perform a brief full-body shake ("Shake it off," we would say), and calmly walk back into her carrier. Even during her physical exams when doctors poked and prodded her, she remained dignified and rarely had anything bad to say.

Administering any medicine orally, though, was a whole different experience. *How dare you attempt to stick that pill into my mouth!* When I needed to do that at home, it was nearly impossible. She became so difficult to handle that I would kneel down behind her to trap her between my legs. As soon as I tried to pop a pill into her mouth, she would complain as loudly as she could and fight back with about twenty paws. Where did they all come from? Even the professionals at the Cat Clinic, who administered feline medication on a daily basis, often needed two or three attempts and occasionally extra hands to get a pill down her throat. On the occasions when I was able to administer medicine successfully, she would run away from me and glare at me from across the room while beating her tail on the floor. *Do not want!*

Buttercup was a better person than I was; she never held a grudge. Within minutes, she would forgive me, and we'd once again be the best of friends. Perhaps she understood that I was really trying to help her.

To make things less traumatic for her, I tried to disguise her medications in food. Sometimes that would work, but usually she could tell. Even when it was a food she really liked, if there was a tiny, crushed-up pill mixed into it, she'd give it a couple of sniffs and walk away. *Yeah, I'm not falling for that.*

She absolutely loved tuna, so whenever I mixed up some tuna salad, I'd let her clean out the can, being sure to leave a few meaty pieces in there for her. The can would get away from her as it slid on the floor or counter top, so I'd often hold it for her until she was done. I tried to use this love of tuna to my advantage. Using a plastic syringe, I would dissolve a pill in the tuna-infused water straight from the can and attempt to squirt the liquid into her mouth. This worked at first, but soon she was on to me.

Later in her life, Buttercup experienced recurring allergies. The only noticeable symptoms were a runny or stuffed up nose and occasional sneezing. When I noticed her nose starting to run, I tried to help her by wiping her face with a tissue. It helped, but she really didn't appreciate it. One of the medications that I attempted to administer a few times was an antihistamine that was supposed to relieve her symptoms. Even though it was only a quarter of a very tiny pill, it was still nearly impossible to get her to take it.

There were also times when her allergy symptoms made her act as though she was attempting to blow her nose or force a sneeze. This occasionally resulted in a bit of a mess, since a cat tends not to cover her face when she sneezes. When she sneezed she was perfectly capable of cleaning herself, but if I could grab a tissue fast enough, I'd still try to help her with it. Once again, she didn't really like that, but later seemed to understand that I was trying to help her.

My feline roommates stayed inside, since indoor cats tend to live much longer and healthier lives than those who venture outdoors. On a rare occasion, one of them might go outside with me wearing a harness and leash. Lily didn't care to go outside at all—she would instantly make her way back to the front door—so I gave up even trying to get her to go out. Bubba was tolerant, but not very fond of the outdoors. He was always on edge, never able to relax while outside. Buttercup was a whole different story. I had to be careful any time I opened a door for fear that she would sneak out. I purchased the harness and leash to help satisfy her desire to be outside and my desire to keep her safe.

Buttercup, being a rather independent cat, didn't particularly care to have a harness put on her. Once the leash was attached and we went outside, she didn't seem to mind the constraint. We would sit on the front stoop and sometimes walk down the steps to the driveway. One time we even went for a "walk" around the block, which consisted mostly of me carrying her, although I set her down occasionally so she could explore. Normally, though, we would stay very close to home, either by the front door or on the deck overlooking the backyard.

When I first purchased the harness, I knew that if any one of the cats could figure out how to escape from it, it would be Buttercup. She was intelligent and persistent —a dangerous combination in a feline. She proved me correct one day. I don't recall if we had been outside and were coming back in or if we were just on our way out, but something spooked her and she got away from me. Fortunately, we were inside and I managed to get the door closed. Seconds later, she contorted her body in a way that only a cat could do and popped free of the harness. This event didn't lessen her desire to be outdoors, however, and soon she became tolerant of the harness because she learned that having it on meant she was about to get a rare opportunity to explore outside, even if it was supervised.

There was one downside of taking Buttercup out on the leash. She was normally a very quiet cat, but after a few minutes of enjoying the world outside the house, she wanted more. Once back inside, she would stand at the door and cry for another outdoor adventure. This would happen off and on for the rest of the day and sometimes into the next. She would become so loud I could hear her from the other side of the house. Figuring something was wrong, I'd go locate her only to find that everything was fine—she just wanted to go outside again.

Living with a cat is no bother. It's just a matter of taking care of his or her needs twenty-four hours a day. One of the needs is managing the litter pans. When Buttercup moved in, I spared no expense. She had a litter pan that was almost fully enclosed for privacy, vented, and had plenty of headroom. It turned out that wasn't the right one, though. Buttercup was a very simple cat, so she decided she didn't need anything that fancy. Once the cover of the fancy box was removed, she was much happier, at least for a while.

Buttercup's first litter pan was in a corner of the kitchen. She must have thought I was crazy. *Who does her business in the kitchen?* She had a way of informing me that it was in the wrong location, and I quickly got the message. I moved the litter pan to a corner of the finished room in the basement. That was wrong, too. Apparently, the correct location was a few feet out from the far wall of that room. Fortunately, that room of the basement was just a storage room and I was flexible, so the pan was moved to her chosen spot. It turned out there was a second spot, too, so I purchased another litter pan. With that, she was finally done arranging the litter pans at her new house.

One winter day, I noticed rodent droppings in the pantry. With three cats in the house, what mouse would dare show its face? I've had mice elsewhere in the house where the cats can't go (the attic) or where they don't go (the garage), but that was the first time I saw evidence of one in the livable space. I cleaned up the droppings, hoping the mouse had already left, but I knew that was unlikely.

The next morning, I found more evidence. I put several traps in place, and the waiting game started. I didn't have to wait very long. That evening, as I was getting ready for bed, I noticed that I was alone. That was odd; normally, at least two cats would have been in the room, or would have already given up on me if I had stayed up too late. Something was up. I went to find them. All three cats were pacing around the refrigerator, looking very intently behind and underneath it: the mouse was back!

I pulled the lower trim plate off the refrigerator but couldn't see anything. I grabbed a yardstick from the pantry and poked it under the refrigerator. On the first attempt, the only things I managed to pull out were inanimate cat toys. On the second pass, though, I flushed out the live mouse. It scurried over to the pantry with all three cats in tow.

Now I had a problem: the mouse was in the pantry, but not in any of the traps. I needed to get into the pantry to try to get the mouse. The cats also wanted to get in, but several still-armed traps were in there. What should I do? I managed to open the pantry and remove the more serious traps before a cat brushed up against them. I then started to remove the other items in the pantry: paper towels, the fire extinguisher, bottles of cleaning solution.

Pretty soon, the mouse shot out of the pantry and ran into the sunken living room.

Now the fun began. Lily and Bubba followed the mouse as far as they could. The mouse ran behind the entertainment center, and then made its way back to the other side of the room to hide behind the sofa. I flushed it out with the yardstick, but had absolutely no plan as to what I would do once it came out. It ran behind the entertainment center again, but since there was no place to hide back there and with two young cats rapidly closing in, it circled back to the sofa. I propped up the opposite end of the sofa so I could get a better look, and once again went at it with the yardstick. Just as before, it scampered across the room, made a pass behind the entertainment center, and returned to the sofa. Lily and Bubba followed it on the complete circuit. This happened several times, but neither Lily nor Bubba caught the mouse. Did they even know how? Apparently, to them, this was all a game. After a while, they grew weary, and they both decided to move on to other more interesting things—like napping and cleaning themselves.

The whole time that Lily, Bubba, and I were going after the mouse, Buttercup had been sitting on the kitchen table, quietly watching the proceedings. When the youngsters got out of the way, she jumped down and came over to look under the sofa. I had lost track of the mouse, but she never did. In fact, any time I couldn't spot it, I just looked at Buttercup and followed her eyes. Her radar was locked on the mouse; she never lost track of the intruder.

Buttercup

She knew exactly what to do. She went around to the side of the sofa where the mouse had been escaping and waited for me to force it out. I did, and the hunt was over before I knew it. With a single pounce, Buttercup showed those other cats how it was done. She carried the mouse to the kitchen and dropped it. The mouse was dazed, but alive.

After praising her for her actions, I located a small Rubbermaid container. Before I could get back to the mouse, it had scampered over to the curtain at the sliding-glass door. Buttercup followed it, but lost track of it as it as it hid behind the drapes before it bolted back out a few feet away. The mouse ran toward the other side of the kitchen. By luck, Bubba happened to be sitting on the floor in front of the stove. I had to credit Bubba with an assist because he made a motion toward the mouse, causing it to turn around and head back in my direction instead of hiding under the stove. That brief hesitation provided me with enough time to slap the container down over the mouse. The rodent was visible through the clear plastic container. Soon, I had three cats orbiting one terrified mouse.

This story has a happy ending for the mouse. With the possible exception of a paw damaged by Buttercup's grip, the mouse appeared to be unharmed. But what does one do with a live mouse trapped under a container? To keep it from escaping, I slid a piece of sheet metal under the container. I took it outside to the dry creek bed behind our house, figuring that was as good a place as any to release a mouse. I removed the metal cover and shook the container, freeing the mouse into the night. In the blue moonlight, I saw the mouse land on a small pile of snow. A few seconds later, it scampered off into the night. That mouse must have told its harrowing story to the other neighborhood mice, because no rodent ever set paw in our house again.

When I took a shower, the bathroom door normally was closed to keep the humidity down in the rest of the house and to prevent the smoke detector from going off. Yes, apparently steam from a shower can activate a smoke detector, especially if the detector is mounted in the hallway right outside the bathroom door. I didn't latch the door, though, just in case any of my feline roommates wanted access to the bathroom. It was easier to do that than to listen to a cat crying on the other side of the door.

If there was suddenly a cold rush of air while I was taking a shower, it was invariably because a cat had pushed the door open. When that happened, I'd reach around the shower curtain and give the door a slight shove to close it again. Occasionally, I needed to close the door two or three times during the course of one shower.

It seemed that Buttercup and Lily had an agreement to keep track of me during my showers. They probably thought I was crazy to go willingly into a place where I'd be sprayed with water, so they needed to make sure I was not harmed. Some days it would be Lily; other days it would be Buttercup. They never came in at the same time, and each had her own way of performing this guard duty. Lily liked to sit or lie on the rug and would start to talk to me as soon as I was done. Buttercup preferred to sit on the edge of the sink and watch me through the translucent shower curtain. Regardless, they both seemed relieved when I safely exited the shower. Lily would arch her back and want me to give her some full head-to-tail petting. If Buttercup were waiting for me, she'd pace along the sink and rub herself against me as soon as I got out.

Whenever Buttercup was on the sink in the bathroom, she would always exit the room the same way. Rather than jumping onto the relatively hard and potentially slippery linoleum, she would jump through the doorway onto the soft carpet in the hallway. I'm not sure why she didn't aim for the plush bathroom rug instead, although perhaps the carpet was a better choice since there was a pad underneath it. It seems she taught this move to the other cats, too. Lily didn't frequent the bathroom sink much, but Bubba was there at least once a day and often executed the same exit maneuver that Buttercup had perfected. Bubba, unlike Buttercup, also occasionally exited the long way, by jumping onto the toilet (fortunately, I kept the lid down) before making his way to the door.

Buttercup's jump from the sink to the hallway floor was very manageable, but some of her other maneuvers frightened me. One of Buttercup's more challenging leaps happened in the hobby room. That room contained a bookcase in the southwest corner, to the right of the entrance to the master bathroom. Due to the combined horizontal and vertical distance, I figured there was no way she could get on top of that bookcase. As usual, though, she proved me wrong. Using the short wall that separated the sink from the rest of the room, along with a thoroughly calculated jump, Buttercup was able to get to the top of that bookcase. This long and difficult leap required all of her strength.

I feared that one miscalculation or slipup would cause her to crash to the floor six feet below. To prevent her from attempting that vault again, I placed an item on top of the bookcase, blocking her landing zone. This didn't stop her from thinking about the jump—she'd often sit on the short wall and look up at the bookcase—but she never attempted that dangerous leap again.

I've always liked the ambiance created by burning candles. Without cats, it was an easy thing to do; with cats, things changed. Buttercup had to check out anything that was new or that she hadn't seen in a while, and a burning candle fell into that category. She was smart enough, however, not to get too close to the flame. As she inched toward it, she would slow down, stare at it briefly, and then back up before eventually turning away. I figured the other cats would be smart enough to stay away from candles, too. There was always a concern, though, of what might happen once they turned away. A long tail flopping back and forth could unintentionally encounter the flame, which could be very dangerous from a fire-control perspective. It would also result in one very upset cat.

It took a bit of searching to come up with cat-safe means of burning candles. Tea lights in votive holders worked fairly well. I found some relatively deep votive holders made from selenite and soapstone. Not only did the flame stay low when a tea light was burned in them, but due to their large mass, a cat could not easily push one off a table. Also, the translucent nature of the stone provided a nice visual effect.

Tea light candles come in a limited variety of scents compared to votive candles, so I was still looking for a solution that would permit me to burn votive and other larger candles. While visiting a local store that sold a variety of unusual things, I came across enclosed metal lanterns in various sizes. The small lanterns could contain a votive holder, while the larger ones could hold multiple votive candles or a single jar candle.

The metal holders weighed less than the stone holders did so they were a bit easier to push around. But the cats tended to avoid them, so it wasn't an issue. Because the flame was completely enclosed, there was never a concern that a stray tail might sweep through it. As a bonus, the patterns in the metal created dazzling light shows on the walls and ceilings. With these holders, I was able to burn candles and the cats were safe.

As she became a senior cat, Buttercup began to develop arthritis. She was smart about it and would not attempt the impressive leaps that she'd made in her younger days. I noticed that instead of jumping straight onto the bathroom sink, she would work her way up there by means of the toilet. Since I kept the lid closed, that was easy for her to do. Similarly, in the kitchen, she would no longer jump straight onto the counter but would start on a chair, jump to the table, and then make the final hop onto the counter. In some places in the house, an option like that wasn't available. I had heard of pet steps, but rather than purchase some I decided to make my own. Having already made a cat tree, I figured a few pet steps would be easy. I fashioned them from plywood and carpet scraps.

Two of the places she liked to go on a daily basis were the bed and the tables in my hobby room. I made a small, two-tier step for the bedroom and a larger, three-tier step for the hobby room. She seemed appreciative, and used them regularly. I wonder if she knew I made them just for her.

Buttercup's routine varied over the years, but one thing was certain: she was always a lap cat. She would go through periods where she would jump on my lap in the morning as I sat on the steps, putting on my shoes. She knew I was getting ready to leave, and she didn't want that. *Shouldn't you stay home and pet the cat?* This would

Buttercup

happen every day for a few weeks and then she'd stop, only to start up again a month or two later.

It can be difficult to tie shoelaces when there is a cat on your lap, especially a wiggly cat. Some days she would jump onto my lap once and stay there for just a few seconds. Other days, she'd jump on and off my lap several times while I attempted to finish tying the laces. But usually she'd jump up once and stay there for as long as she could. And, of course, she had me wrapped around her little paw, so I'd give in every time. This made me late on a few occasions.

With my regular job, this was not an issue, as I normally work autonomously and could easily adjust my schedule. With my weekend volunteer position at the animal shelter, it would cause a problem. When people are counting on me, I pride myself on being prompt. I value the other volunteers' time, and since I'm the one with the key for the shelter on my day, I like to arrive before they do so that their time isn't wasted.

One day, Buttercup decided she needed a serious amount of attention before I left. That made me several minutes late. When I arrived covered in fur, two of the other volunteers were waiting for me. "Sorry I'm late," I said. "It's because of a female. She refused to get off me this morning until I gave her lots of lovin'." They chuckled, knowing it had to be Buttercup.

She wasn't the only cat that ever made me late. Lily delayed my trip to work one day and may have saved my life in the process. My team was in the final stages of a product release, so a lot of our test equipment was in high demand. To maximize our use of the limited number of test stations, we decided to run a split schedule; half of the team would come in two hours later than normal and stay later while the other half would come in two hours early and leave early. This permitted us to collaborate when necessary but also made it easier for all of us to get time on a test station.

I was in the "early" group that was to arrive at 6:00 a.m. That freed up more time in the afternoon and seemed like less of an interruption in my normal routine. Not being a "morning person" made the start of the day a bit challenging for me, though. Rather than arriving at the desired time, I was showing up between 6:05 and 6:15, and once even as late as 6:30. One evening I decided that the following day I would make it to work by 6:00 no matter what. With my alarm adjusted, I went to bed a bit earlier in order to make it easier to get up in the morning. When the alarm went off, I was ready to jump up, but Lily had other plans for me. She decided to leap onto the bed and lie down on my chest. She purred loudly and demanded my attention in a way that she had never done before. Despite wanting to meet my 6:00 a.m. arrival goal, I just couldn't say no to her. Stroking her long fur, I wondered why she was so interested in me that morning. Normally, she only showed interest in me in the morning if her food dishes were empty, and typically, she did that by walking across me repeatedly.

After a few minutes, she decided that she was done, so she jumped from the bed, leaving as quickly as she had arrived. I immediately sprang out of bed and began my morning routine. There was still some food left in the cats' dishes, which made her behavior even stranger. I cleaned and refilled the food and water dishes, wondering what had gotten into her.

I left for work feeling good because I'd be there soon after 6:00, but resigned myself to the fact that I hadn't met my goal. It was still dark as I entered the westbound side of the divided highway for my eight-mile commute. At least there was a lot less traffic that early in the morning than there was during my normal commute time. Lily's strange behavior faded from my thoughts as I began to focus on the day's work. Approximately three miles from my destination, I crested a hill, when suddenly something seemed wrong. Very wrong. I couldn't make out what I was looking at. In the distance there were lights where there shouldn't be lights, on both sides of the westbound lanes. Instinctively, I began to slow down. There were taillights in the middle of the road, straddling the centerline. A few seconds later, as I got closer to the lights, I figured out what I was looking at: the side of an eighteen-wheeler. It was stopped at an angle, blocking both lanes and parts of both shoulders. The taillights that I had seen in the center of the road were those of a car wedged underneath the trailer. The top of the car had been sheared off in the collision.

There were no emergency vehicles in sight—this wreck had just happened a minute or two before. A handful of people milled about but they didn't seem too concerned. I didn't have a cell phone at the time, and none of the people flagged me down, so I figured the best thing I could do was to leave the area. I did not want to be in the way, especially since there was more traffic coming up behind me. A couple of miles down the road, I saw the first emergency responders headed toward the scene of the wreck. They were from a fire station close to my employer.

That evening, I learned from a local news source that the driver of the truck had attempted to make a U-turn from the eastbound lanes to the westbound lanes at one of the connecting medians. As dangerous and illegal as that was, it was especially bad for a vehicle of that size, on the backside of a hill, in the dark. I also learned that the driver of the car did not survive.

Based on where the responding emergency vehicle was relative to the fire station, and how long it took me to see it after driving past the wreck, I estimated that the wreck had happened two or three minutes before I got there—about the same amount of time that Lily had delayed me in the morning. Did she know? She had never acted like that before, nor did she exhibit that behavior again. But that particular day, she seemed very intent on keeping me in bed a few extra minutes.

I didn't travel often, but any time I did, Buttercup was always the first to figure it out. Even when I tried to hide my impending trip by packing the suitcase without her seeing it and keeping it hidden in the closet, she always figured it out. She was probably noticing the other things that I did in preparation for a trip. As I got things ready, she would sit in the hallway and watch me. *You're leaving again, aren't you?*

Upon my return, Buttercup would often act very aloof for the first few hours. *Oh, it's you. Were you gone?* As I unpacked, I often wouldn't see much of her, but by sundown, she would be back to her habit of absorbing as much lap time as possible.

Mutual Grooming

Chapter 10: It's Good to be Queen

Cat society is hierarchical. One day while my parents were visiting, they asked about the pecking order in my house. I replied that Buttercup was the alpha cat, followed by me, then Bubba, and finally Lily. They were surprised that Bubba outranked Lily, since he was much younger and newer to the family. For some reason, they didn't question my being outranked by Buttercup.

It wasn't always like that; I was definitely the "top cat" when Buttercup moved in. It's not clear exactly when that changed, although I suspect Buttercup decided she needed to exert control over the house around the time that Lily moved in.

Buttercup was a very good alpha cat. It was odd, as she was the smallest of the three cats, but she was there first. Often, though not always, the first cat in a house becomes the alpha cat. What made Buttercup such a good leader was that she only used force when she deemed it necessary. She ruled with an iron paw, but a heart of gold. Both Lily and Bubba respected her supreme authority.

Lily never really presented a problem for her, although there were times when Buttercup had to remind her who was in charge. Lily would often be energetic and playful when Buttercup just wanted to relax. When Lily was an adolescent, I had to close the bedroom door, locking her out of the room on a few nights, just so Buttercup and I could get some sleep.

Lily pretty much always knew she was outranked by Buttercup. Bubba, on the other hand, frequently needed to be schooled on who was in charge, at least for the first few years. Bubba had been quarantined in the unfinished room of the basement when he first moved in, but once his test results for feline leukemia and FIV came back negative, we allowed him to explore more of the house. Lily was the first cat he met. She had been concerned about the mysterious cat on the other side of the door, so she was right there and got to meet him as soon as the door was opened. If Lily wanted to be in control, she messed up the instant she saw him. When the door to Bubba's room was opened, he slowly crept into the room where Lily and I were waiting. As soon as he did, Lily turned and ran toward the far corner of the room. From that instant, at the mighty age of twelve weeks, Bubba was dominant over Lily.

Bubba seemed to fit into his new home just fine, but Lily needed some time to adjust to this expanded family, for she was no longer the youngest cat in the house. Right after Bubba gained free run of the house, Lily started spending nearly all her time in the unfinished basement where Bubba had stayed. I would go down to talk to her and give her attention, but she wouldn't leave that room. After about a week of pouting, she seemed to realize two things: first, Bubba was here to stay; and second, I still loved her and would make time to socialize with her. She also seemed to mature a lot in that week. She wasn't nearly as obnoxious as she had been before, although she was still playful and talkative.

Buttercup was quite accepting of Bubba, just as she had been of Lily. Buttercup rarely had to discipline Lily, but there were many times she had to put her paw down with Bubba. This was strange and entertaining to watch because she had always been such an easy-going cat. Taking on this distinctly dominant role was a side of her I hadn't seen.

Soon after Bubba moved in, I saw him pin Lily down while biting her scruff. Lily would typically just accept this show of force, although she might complain a bit. Eventually she'd work a hind paw out and start to kick at him, after which he would jump off.

A few days later, I was working in my hobby room while Buttercup was sprawled on her back on the floor close to me. She was still in that very submissive and vulnerable position when Bubba walked into the room and saw what he thought was an easy target. He walked over and sat, looking down on her. Buttercup barely moved a muscle. She didn't get up. Instead, she stared him down, giving him one of the nastiest looks I'd ever seen. She also began beating her tail on the floor. Bubba may have been young, but he got the message: *Don't mess with the queen!* He stood up, turned around, and left the room. It's fascinating the way they were able to communicate with each other so clearly.

That's not to say he didn't try to usurp the throne once in a while. Often in his younger days, he would run toward Buttercup with an apparent attack in mind, and then veer off at the last second. *Just kidding!*

Most of the time, Buttercup shrugged off this annoying little ball of fur, but there were a few times she had to take action. It was quite amusing to see Buttercup's sweet, kind nature take a backseat when her boss-lady side came out. If Bubba were being extra annoying, she would stand over him and stare down with a look of disgust and anger. On more than one occasion, she had to bop him on the head. Early on, he would hide behind me when that happened, but I'd tell him, "Hey, you asked for it! I'm not going to fight your battles." Later, when he annoyed Buttercup and she started to discipline him, he would instantly lie down, expose his belly, and become submissive.

As Bubba grew to be a large and muscular cat in excess of thirteen pounds, he still respected Buttercup's authority. The few times he didn't, she knocked him down a notch or two. Even in Buttercup's final months when she weighed less than six pounds, she demonstrated that she was still clearly in control. One evening while I was scooping litter pans, Bubba apparently did something to upset her. She took off after him and chased him out of the room. Seconds later, he ran back into the room. She was still running after him, letting him know who was in charge. I was so proud of her.

As she ruled her house, Buttercup carried herself with an aura of confidence. She was very definitive; she never second-guessed herself. She would check out anything and everything I did without hesitation. When she figured out how to get to the top of the entertainment center, she did so with purpose. She lived by the principle that it never hurts to ask for what you want, and normally she got it. If she wanted to get up high on a shelf or into a cubbyhole, she would do it. She was half the size of Bubba but she never feared him: this was *her* house. She decided she was in charge, and nothing would change that. Her confidence made her a well-respected leader. That confidence was very visible the day she had to defend her territory from a dog twice her size.

The way Buttercup handled the neighbor's small but very loud and annoying dog compared with how Bubba reacted demonstrated the uniqueness of each cat. Anytime I was outside and the neighbors let their dog out, she would run up to me and bark nonstop, "*Yap! Yap! Yap! Yap!*" That dog would just keep barking until one of her humans summoned her back into the house.

Although Bubba wasn't as enamored with the outside world as Buttercup was, Bubba would occasionally go outside on the leash with me. One day Bubba and I were outside on the front steps when the neighbors let their dog out. She ran straight toward Bubba and me, barking wildly as usual. Having never seen a dog up close, Bubba went berserk. He flipped over backwards and lost bladder control while he attempted to make his way back to the front door. We managed to get back inside and eventually he settled down. Fortunately, he was not permanently traumatized by that event.

A few weeks later, I was outside with Buttercup in the driveway when the neighbors once again let their canine monstrosity outside to take care of business. As usual, as soon as she saw me she started barking and ran right over to me. This time, though, things were different. Buttercup's behavior was the complete opposite of Bubba's. She hunkered down slightly, but otherwise stood her ground and stared the canine down. The dog didn't know what to make of this, apparently never having met a cat that wouldn't run from her. I'd never seen that dog shut up so quickly! She stopped barking, cocked her head sideways, and took a few steps back while looking at Buttercup. My sweetheart didn't move. Flustered by this lack of response, the dog ran back to her own yard with her tail between her legs, and without any more barking. Buttercup continued to stare her down until she was out of sight. *Who does that dog think she is? This is* my *territory!*

Despite being the alpha cat, Buttercup was very good at sharing things. When Lily was only a year or two old, she would jump to the top of the small cat tree in the hobby room even when—or perhaps especially when—Buttercup was there. Buttercup was quite accepting of this even as Lily stretched out, poking and prodding at her. I have a photo showing Buttercup being very tolerant of this behavior even though she has a *why me?* expression on her face. Later, when I added the big cat tree to the living room, Buttercup did a nice job of sharing it with Lily. She didn't care which spot Lily took as long as Lily wasn't disturbing her.

Buttercup was also good at sharing my chair with Bubba. When he was young, there were several instances when Buttercup was lying on the chair, paws comfortably tucked underneath her, and Bubba decided that the chair was the place to be. He jumped up, inevitably causing the seat to spin briefly, and then sat or lay down next to her. She easily could have booted him off, but she was very accepting of him, and since he wasn't really bothering her, she let him be. She always chose her battles carefully, and didn't let the unimportant issues get under her skin. Besides, Bubba would groom her on the chair.

With multiple cats, mutual grooming sometimes took place. All three of the cats would groom the others, but Lily was especially interested in grooming the other two. She liked to groom Bubba on the bed. In one of the few circumstances in which she appeared to be more dominant than Bubba, she would hold him down with one or both front paws while licking his fur. She liked to groom Buttercup, too, but normally wouldn't try to restrain her. I noticed that Buttercup would appear to request—or more likely, *demand*—that Lily clean her. She would approach Lily and lower her head slightly. *Groom me, servant.* She would never make contact with Lily, but instead waited for Lily to start licking the fur on top of her head. Lily always obeyed. Although Buttercup would try to groom Lily occasionally, it seemed that Lily preferred to do the grooming while Buttercup appreciated the service.

Chapter 11: Cat Tales

Throughout her years, Buttercup did a variety of things that surprised or amazed me. Over time, I learned never to underestimate her intelligence or persistence.

One of the greatest joys of living with Buttercup was that she would always come to bed with me. Especially when I wasn't feeling well, it was nice to know that someone was there by my side. Waking in the middle of the night and feeling her leaning against my back was one of the nicest things I've ever experienced.

We were both creatures of habit, so we had a regular bedtime routine. While getting ready for bed one evening, I noticed she wasn't in the room. That seemed a bit unusual, but I went to bed anyway. After all, she was an independent cat, so maybe she was just out doing cat stuff. After a few minutes, she still hadn't shown up. The more I thought about it, the more something didn't seem right; she *always* came to bed with me. I decided to call her.

"Buttercup!"

"*Merrrow!*" came a muffled response from somewhere down the hallway. I waited briefly but she didn't show up.

"Buttercup!" I tried again.

"*Murrow.*"

Still no cat appeared in my bedroom. Something wasn't right.

"Buttercup?"

"*Mprroww!*"

Something was definitely wrong. She wasn't a very talkative cat, and she sounded concerned. The fact that she responded to me but didn't come to bed was enough to get me to investigate. I flipped various lights on and made my way to the end of the hallway. Proceeding down the half flight of stairs to the front door, I turned the foyer light on and found her sitting on the top of the staircase that led to the basement. She was looking in my direction, but didn't seem interested in me.

"What's wrong?" I asked, as if I expected her to answer. Surprisingly, that's exactly what she did.

"*Mreow,*" she replied softly, as she jumped up to the main level. She walked over to where I had set my bag down after work and began pawing under it. I lifted the bag to find a cockroach crawling around in circles.

"Keep an eye on him, sweetie!" I said as I ran to the kitchen to get a flyswatter and some paper towels. The bug hustled about, looking for an escape route, but Buttercup was able to keep it in check.

When I came back, I said, "OK, step back." Surprisingly, she took a couple of steps back and I was able to whack the bug with the flyswatter. After disposing of it with a paper towel, I praised her for a job well done and encouraged her to come to bed.

I crawled into bed and waited for her, figuring if anything else was wrong she'd let me know. She made her security rounds one more time. Minutes later, with her job done, she checked in for the night, stretching out next to me in bed.

I was surprised when I arrived at home one day and found a loaf of bread on the living room floor. How did it get there? I kept the bread on top of the refrigerator about twenty feet away. Someone had to have carried or dragged it clear across the kitchen, then down a step to the sunken living room. Surely, Buttercup couldn't have done that, but at the time she was the only cat in the house. She certainly had to be responsible for the kitty-mouth-sized teeth marks in the plastic bag. How could she have gotten to it? The top of the refrigerator wasn't accessible to a cat. It was in the corner of the kitchen with a wall on one side and a small counter and cabinet on the other. The counter held a microwave, and it was barely big enough for that.

Being a cat, Buttercup certainly could jump, but not high enough to get to the top of the microwave. Or so I thought. There had to be way she got up there, but I couldn't figure it out.

The mystery was solved a few days later when Buttercup decided to fess up and show me her trick. Only a small sliver of countertop was exposed in front of the microwave. That wasn't enough for a cat to jump to and land securely, but she could jump on it and use it as a springboard to get to the top of the microwave. From there it was an easy hop to the top of the refrigerator. That meant I no longer could store bread or anything else edible there. I don't know if she ever got up there again, but I don't think she did. Getting there required a lot of strength and well-calculated jumps, so once she learned that nothing worthwhile was kept there anymore, it was no longer worth the effort. A few years later, I began storing items up there again, and nothing was ever disturbed.

Bread wasn't the only large thing she dragged a significant distance. While getting ready for work one day, I noticed that only one of my shoes was by the front door. Where could the other one be? Buttercup had recently discovered the joys of playing with shoelaces, and had once dragged one of my shoes a few feet, but now one shoe was completely missing. After a little searching, I discovered the missing shoe halfway down the staircase to the basement. I didn't think it was possible for a cat her size to drag a shoe that far, but then again, she had managed to move an entire loaf of bread halfway across the house. As persistent and intelligent as she was, by that point I figured she could do just about anything she set her mind to. Later, I gave Buttercup her own shoelace toys. After that, she would play with hers and leave mine alone. They were the only things she played with for her whole life, long after losing interest in other toys.

It was nice to be greeted when I arrived home. Normally, the cats were by the door waiting for me in their usual locations. So the day that I arrived home and found no one on the other side of the door, I knew something was up. Lily had recently moved in, doubling the number of cats that should have been waiting for me. I went into my normal routine of scooping the litter pans, but down in the basement there was surprisingly little evidence that the pans had been used. Upstairs in the kitchen, the food dishes also were hardly touched. That was when I started to get worried. I decided to go upstairs to check the bedrooms, but as I rounded the corner in the hallway, I saw that the bathroom door was completely closed. Upon opening it, I found two very grateful kitties who had learned to live with each other over the course of several hours. Based on the food and litter pan evidence, I estimated it must have been no later than mid morning when they ended up in the bathroom. At that time, Lily was still trying to determine her place in the house and was occasionally obnoxious with Buttercup. I suspected that once they were confined to the bathroom, they had scuffled, pushing the door closed hard enough to get it to latch. By the time I arrived, they had worked out their issues and were happy to eat dinner side by side.

After the bathroom incident, Buttercup and Lily became tolerant of each other. Not only would there be periods of mutual grooming, but one day I walked into the dining room to find Buttercup resting her head on Lily's soft, furry back. However, most of the time, they just ignored each other and each did her own thing. Normally, they wouldn't even sit next to each other, especially if I tried to put them together.

One evening, though, I was able to put them side by side, and it didn't bother them. There was a heck of a ruckus outside the living room window adjacent to the small cat tree. The window overlooked the lattice roof atop the patio. Standing on the lattice was a moderately large bird, tearing into a meal of the small rodent it held in its talons. "Oh, this is something the girls would love to see!" I thought. I grabbed Buttercup and placed her on the cat tree. She instantly froze and became immersed in this incredible nature show on cat TV. I also found Lily and placed her on the cat tree. Normally, the top of the cat tree was only big enough for one cat, but with their attention focused on this exciting event taking place, I don't think either of them was even aware of the other.

It is well known that cats have very sensitive hearing. Buttercup was no exception. She became especially attuned to the sound my office chair would make as I sat down. Regardless of where she was in the house, it seemed that whenever I sat down in that chair, she would materialize and find her way to my lap. Not wanting to disturb her once she was settled, I learned to prepare to settle in before taking my seat. This involved making sure that anything I would want for the next hour—say a drink, a book, or the remote control—was within reach of that chair. It was also good to have the brush nearby. Buttercup normally didn't care to be brushed and would try to sneak away when the brushing started. When necessary, though, I could work in a few strokes of the brush as she sat on my lap. Fortunately, she took excellent care of her fur and did not require extensive brushing.

Buttercup would often walk in front of me when I used the computer, as many cats apparently do. Sometimes this involved walking or sitting on the keyboard. One of my computer tables didn't offer much room between the keyboard and the edge of the table, so it was difficult for her to walk or sit there. When she tried to sit, she would almost invariably end up pressing a key. When I saw that was about to happen, I would try move the keyboard out of the way to prevent erratic behavior on the computer. Due to limited space, about the only thing I could do was tilt the keyboard up and stand it on its side. Buttercup did not seem at all concerned that she was preventing me from getting any work done. Rather, she would stare at me as if to say, *Look at me—LOOK AT ME! It's time to play with the cat!* Her tail would be draped over the edge of the table, its tip slowly but endlessly twitching. With that look on her face, how could I say no? I'd start to stroke her back and a nasty case of elevator-butt would come over her.

One day, Buttercup decided to sit on the keyboard of my Linux computer. I had a terminal window open, and before I could safely move the pointer to activate a harmless window, a kitty butt was on my keyboard. Somehow, she managed to sit on the up-arrow, which scrolled through the history of previously entered commands. Her position on the keyboard was apparently a bit uncomfortable, so she adjusted herself and then sat down again. Now off the keyboard, she looked at me intently as if she was trying to tell me something. "What?" I asked. Then I looked at the terminal window and read the command on which she had stopped. I couldn't believe what I saw: it said, "cat hi."

How did she do that? A few days earlier, I had apparently typed the command, "cat hi," to see what the file named "hi" contained. In a Linux or Unix operating system, the command "cat," short for *concatenate*, is a tool that is used to combine files. If the output is not redirected to a new file, then it goes to the standard output device, which is typically a terminal window on the screen. As such, one common use for this command is to display the contents of a single file by typing "cat" followed by the file name. What were the odds that I would have had a file named "hi," *and* had wanted to see its contents, *and* Buttercup had landed on the up-arrow to scroll back through the commands, *and* she had released the key exactly when the command "cat hi" was displayed? I knew it was all just a freak coincidence, yet as I looked into her eyes I couldn't help but think that perhaps she was much smarter than anyone imagined.

Bubba always had a thing for my chair. When he joined the family as a kitten, he was quarantined for a bit, but the day I let him have full access to the house, he spent about half an hour doing some unsupervised roaming and then found me in the hobby room. He jumped onto my chair, which I think he then declared to be *his* chair, and curled up for a nap as if he had been here his whole life. Not wanting to disturb him, I decided to sit in the guest chair.

One day when he was a bit older, the two tabbies conspired against me. As I was settling in to do some work in the hobby room, I briefly got up from my chair. Bubba frequently waited for me to get up from *his* chair so that he could jump onto it. After all, the only thing better than sleeping on a chair is sleeping on a chair that someone else wants to use. I was barely up when Bubba sprang onto the chair. D'oh! "OK, no problem," I thought, as I simply grabbed the guest chair and moved it over to the table. Then I remembered something else that I needed, so I left the room. Returning less than a minute later, I discovered Buttercup had occupied the second chair! Maybe the number of chairs I needed equaled the number of cats in the house plus one? I then procured a chair from the office/storage room across the hall. Even if I decided to get up, there was no need to worry about *that* chair becoming occupied, since Lily was never interested in sitting on chairs.

Can cats see things that we humans can't? Perhaps when a cat sits and stares intently into nothing, it's because there's actually something very interesting to see.

The large black tomcat that we had when I was young had a very strange experience one evening. I was doing homework as he walked into my bedroom; suddenly, he screamed, and there was a huge commotion. I looked in his direction and saw him cowering while staring upward, wide-eyed, with the most terrified expression on his face. He frantically backed up, flipped over backwards, and ran out of the room. Thinking something had to be wrong, I went to look for him. I found him on the lower level at the other end of the house, sitting in the middle of a room, frozen like a statue. He seemed unharmed, but he refused leave that spot for several hours. What did he see that frightened him so much?

On occasion, Buttercup stared off into space as if she were focusing on something. One day while my parents were visiting, Buttercup sat on a corner of the coffee table and stared toward the open doorway to the dining room. My mother asked, "What does she see?" There was nothing there.

Several years later, as I was about ready to go to bed one night, I heard Buttercup meow from the hallway. It seemed a bit odd and was reminiscent of the cockroach incident, so I decided to check it out. I found her near the end of the hallway.

"What is it?" I said.

She took a few steps forward and meowed softly a couple of times while looking up toward the middle of the hallway. She appeared to focus on the space between us, four or five feet off the floor. My grandmother Lenore had died the previous day. A thought entered my mind: was Buttercup reacting to her spirit as she stopped by to check on me? Since nothing seemed to be wrong, I went to bed. Soon, Buttercup joined me. I never saw her react that way again.

Since we lived several hundreds of miles apart, Buttercup and my grandmother never had a chance to meet. That was unfortunate, because they had so much in common. Not only were they both short, petite, polite, and soft-spoken, but like my grandmother, Buttercup was a strong, fiercely independent, well-respected matriarch who was dearly loved by those around her.

Not all cats respond to catnip in the same manner. Some cats go crazy while others don't react at all. Even with just three cats, I'd seen a wide variety of behaviors when I broke out the catnip. Lily was the lightweight—just a brief whiff of the stuff and she would be rolling on the floor and begging for more. Bubba was the complete opposite; he'd show a little interest, but did little more than sniff it. Buttercup was right in the middle—she enjoyed some recreational catnip, but knew where to draw the line. If I sprinkled some on the kitchen floor, she'd alternate between licking it and briefly rolling in it. She'd have fun but would never let her guard down.

To help bring new life into old toys, I would keep some of the fuzzy balls and mice sealed in a container with a bunch of catnip. The toys would soak up the aroma of the mint, and bits of the plant would stick to them. Every so often, I would open the container and present some of the wonderfully scented toys to the cats. Both Buttercup and Lily loved this and would play with the toys for quite some time. Bubba showed some interest but not nearly as much as the girls did. They would roll around on the floor while smelling, licking, and batting at the toys. Lily would often want to play with whichever toy Buttercup had. To keep this game going, I always put a few more toys in the container whenever I took some out.

I kept the catnip container in a built-in cabinet in the dining room. Whenever I opened one of the cabinet doors or drawers, both Buttercup and Lily would become very interested in what I was doing. Was it because the catnip was stored there? Or was it because these were places they normally couldn't explore? I had to open this cabinet carefully for fear that one of them would jump up and start to knock things over. Even if neither of the girls was around when I opened one of those drawers, their sensitive hearing could pick up that sound no matter where they were in the house, and within seconds they'd be standing at my feet.

The cabinet containing the catnip also had a couple of drawers. As with the cabinet doors, the girls were fascinated by the drawers. On a couple of occasions I removed the drawers in order to access the wall cavity behind the cabinet for the installation of wires and pipe for a central vacuum system. Fearful that a cat might jump into the opening, I made sure that Buttercup and the others were secured elsewhere in the house while performing that work.

Of the three cats in my life, Buttercup was the only one that didn't have any really bad habits. Both Lily and Bubba had some bad habits that also left their marks on the house.

Lily would scratch the wood trim, which was quite an accomplishment, since she only had her back claws. When she'd get fired up, she would jump and grab a doorframe or a baluster, howl to whoever would listen, and leave scratch marks as she slid backwards. Some of these scratch marks were several feet off the ground. It was surprising that she could get that high, given her weight.

Lily also drooled. The more content she was when being petted, the more she'd slobber. This was a bit annoying when she would lie on top of me in bed. As I would pet her in the morning while she attempted to draw attention to the fact that I hadn't yet served her breakfast, she'd start to drip on me. She would purr softly while I gave her chin rubs and as much petting as she'd like, but soon there would be cat drool on my hand, arms, pajamas, or blankets.

Bubba also had a few unsavory habits. One day he started spraying around the house. Why he was doing that was a mystery until one evening when I heard a commotion in the basement. Bubba was on the perch by the door, freaking out and pounding on the glass. Outside on the patio, staring back at him, was a small black cat. This cat was invading his territory and he was mad! Soon I started to draw a correlation between the frequency of his spraying and how often this stray showed up. Dr. Schomacker at the Cat Clinic said there was a good chance his behavior was a reaction to the intruder.

Less annoying, but possibly a bit more disgusting, was the fact that Bubba liked to eat tissues. Why is a tissue so tasty? Since they couldn't be good for his digestive system, I did everything I could to keep tissues out of his reach.

Buttercup was much too dignified to do any of these things. The worst habit she had was being *extremely* demanding of lap time, but unlike being slobbered on or picking up half-eaten tissues, lap time with Buttercup was very enjoyable.

There was one annoying thing that Buttercup occasionally did: she'd pull the kitchen wastebasket over. The scavenger in her was always looking for a tasty treat. Whenever I heard a crash, I'd go to investigate. Almost invariably, I'd find the waste bin toppled over and Buttercup wearing an expression that suggested she knew she was busted. She was just doing what came naturally to her, though, so there was no point in getting upset. After picking up any spilled garbage, I'd tie the bag, move it to the garage, and then put a new bag in the bin. This didn't happen often, mostly because Buttercup trained me never to put any tempting food scraps in the trashcan. Whenever I found the bin pulled over, it was usually because she had gone after something that I never suspected she'd find enticing.

Her next-worst habit was her unhealthy fascination with rubber bands and twist ties. I learned early on that my bin of rubber bands needed to be placed somewhere inaccessible to her; otherwise, she would start to chew on them. Some cats have been known to eat them, which is something best avoided. As far as I know, Buttercup never actually ate one, but I had to take them away from her forcefully a few times.

I often used twist ties to keep unused cables organized. As I worked on various projects, I would sometimes temporarily remove the ties, but keep them for reuse. I had to be very careful when I set one down, lest quiet, stealthy Buttercup would swoop in and grab it. The pieces of metal wire in twist ties were not good for her teeth or diet, so whenever I removed one, I needed to place it where she couldn't reach it. If I didn't immediately do that, she would hunt it down in the blink of an eye.

It was amazing at how quickly she could find them even when she was out of the room and didn't see me remove it. If I nonchalantly set a twist tie down on a table with other items, within seconds of walking into the room Buttercup could somehow manage to locate it. She normally didn't bother my stuff, so when I noticed her sitting on the table showing an interest in something, or worse, chewing on something, an immediate investigation was in order. She'd give me a disgusted expression when I took it away from her. *Hey, I wasn't done with that!*

There was one other item that intrigued Buttercup: a small white eraser. It was one of the things she would start to push around when she wanted me to play with her. Surprisingly, I found a way to hide it in plain sight. The eraser was less than half an inch thick and about three-quarters of an inch square. Its corners were rounded from use. It was also about the same size, shape, and color as the keys on the keyboard of my Linux computer. One day after she got my attention by playing with the eraser, I placed it in an empty spot on the keyboard when she wasn't looking. It fit perfectly between the escape key and the "F1" key, and blended in as if it were just another key. I kept it there for over ten years, and despite all the times she walked by that keyboard, she never again bothered it. She would occasionally bat at the pens and pencils that I kept at the top of the keyboard, but she completely ignored that eraser. For once, I outsmarted her!

The only other issue, one that all the cats were guilty of, was eating plants. When I moved into the house, I put some impatiens and a jade plant in the plant window and placed a palm in a much larger pot at the front window. Each cat that entered my life decided to eat one type of plant. Buttercup started that trend, pretty much demolishing my impatiens, but always left the others alone. A few years later, Lily destroyed the palm. After Bubba moved in, I started to notice little teeth marks on the jade's leaves. At that point, I decided to put up a battle to defend my jade. Using some wire mesh, I created a barrier to the upper shelf of the plant window while leaving the lower shelf open. Buttercup was still able to enjoy sunning herself in the warm window, and the jade was safe from Bubba. It worked so well that I would occasionally add other plants to the window.

The High Ground

Chapter 12: On the Prowl

Buttercup's passion in life may have been lap time, but a close second was her desire to explore. There wasn't a square inch of her house that she hadn't inspected. It also didn't matter how much or how frequently she explored, she'd still go on the prowl to keep an eye on every bit of her territory. If she thought she needed to get somewhere that was inaccessible due to a closed door, she'd let me know. It didn't matter that nothing ever changed behind any of those closed doors—she simply needed to check.

When Buttercup first moved in, she was fascinated with the garage. She had entirely explored her new home, but the garage was a part of her territory that she couldn't reach. What was a cat to do? I learned to be very careful any time the door to the garage was opened. She was lightning fast and knew how to get out of my reach. If she bolted past me, she would dive under the truck, where she knew I couldn't grab her.

I employed various methods to get her out of there. After all, a garage just isn't a safe place for a cat. Sometimes I used a long object to encourage her to get out from underneath the vehicle. Other times I acted as if I hadn't even noticed she was there, hoping she would let her guard down and come out to explore. That worked a few times. Although I didn't like doing this, a couple of times I left the door to the house open so she had a clean shot to safety, and after ensuring she was on the ground and not climbing around on the truck, I started the engine, hoping the loud sound would startle her into retreating to the house. That also worked a few times. But a human can never out-stubborn a cat. One winter day I just gave up, shut the door, and went into the house. I went back a short while later to find that she was very eager to leave the unheated garage and come inside.

To help appease her desire to explore the garage, I occasionally carried her out there in my arms. I kept telling her there was nothing in the garage for a kitty, but she wouldn't believe me. This way, she was safe but could still see whatever it was she needed to see. Even better, this permitted her to be outside the living space of the house without wearing the uncomfortable harness.

Although she normally didn't care to be picked up—she was a cat, after all, so getting that close to a human had to be *her* idea—she didn't seem to mind being confined to my arms as we explored the fascinating garage. As she grew older, she started to realize that the garage was a cold and boring place and her desire to go out there diminished. Eventually, she lost all interest in it.

The only thing better than going into the garage, which was almost like going outside, was actually going outside. Buttercup would look for any opportunity to do that. In Buttercup's house, there were three ways to go outdoors: the front door, the sliding-glass door in the basement, and the sliding-glass door in the kitchen. If I opened any of these doors, Buttercup would materialize out of nowhere.

The sliding-glass door between the kitchen and the deck made a unique sound, which, while not very loud, could be heard throughout the house by a cat with sensitive hearing. Buttercup would run to the kitchen any time I opened the door—or more correctly, any time I opened the curtain that covered the door. This was especially true after I made the mistake of carrying her out on the deck one warm spring day. After that, she assumed that any time that door was opened, she was going to go explore her deck.

The deck was at the southwest corner of the house. It received a lot of sunshine, so it was a great place to brew sun tea. I placed the gallon jug right outside the door so I wouldn't even have to walk out on the deck for a glass of tea, which was nice on those one hundred-plus-degree summer days. Care had to be used while moving a gallon jug of water and tea bags past one very determined cat. Buttercup always kept an eye on what was happening in the kitchen, so even as the jug was filling with water, she probably knew that the deck door would soon open. On the rare occasion that she was preoccupied with something else, permitting me to prepare the tea for brewing without her noticing, she'd come running as soon as she heard that curtain move or the door slide open.

Buttercup would often play the role of my shadow—she followed me everywhere. Nothing happened in her house without her supervision. That was especially true if I was working in a part of the house where I normally didn't spend much time, such as the basement. There was a small workshop in the unfinished utility room in the basement. When working in there, I would close the door for her safety. She'd be on the other side of that door waiting for me, and she'd usually cry at me through the door. *Why can't I come in there? I need to see what's going on! You need to be supervised!*

One location to which she never gained access was the attic. Access to my attic was through a hatch located in the closet in the hobby room. Getting into it required a six-foot stepladder. One day after working in the attic all morning, I came down briefly and forgot to close the door to the hobby room. Even though I was only away for a couple of minutes, when I returned, I found Buttercup at the top of the ladder, peering into the open hole in the ceiling. Fortunately, she didn't jump up there. The attic was unfinished, and she probably would have created quite the mess in the blown-in cellulose insulation. After all, the mess I normally created was bad enough, despite trying my hardest to keep things clean.

Whether I was working or playing, Buttercup insisted on inspecting everything I did. While partaking in any of my hobbies, Buttercup would be there. As I prepared rockets for a day of flying, Buttercup would be right there. After a day of flying them at the local park or with a rocket club, I would come home and clean up my equipment. Of course, Buttercup would be there watching.

Building rockets? Buttercup was there. I had to be careful when it came time to use epoxy. Wrapping Christmas gifts? Buttercup would help. Folding and putting away clothes? She was there. Using the bathroom? She'd be sitting on the sink. Rebuilding a computer? Buttercup whiskers would be probing inside the case. Doing anything with papers? You bet Buttercup was there—probably sprawled out on them. Wiping down the kitchen counter after washing the dishes? Buttercup was there. (More paw prints? I just cleaned that counter!)

Of course, whenever I had any cupboard, drawer, or closet open, she had to inspect it. After all, it was part of her territory, and a part that was normally off-limits. I tried to fight it at first when it came to the kitchen cupboards, but eventually I just gave in. When I opened a cupboard to take out a pan, I'd leave the door open so she could perform her inspection. It was just easier that way. For some reason, the cupboard next to the sink that held crackers and boxes of teas was incredibly interesting to her. First, she'd check out the lower level; after it passed inspection, she'd put her paws on the upper shelf and determine whether the opening was big enough for her to make the jump. It normally wasn't, but that didn't stop her. Boxes of tea bags would invariably fall to the floor. Eventually, I got the hint and repositioned things so it was easier for her to take care of her inspection duties.

Another cupboard that interested her was the one to the right of the sink, above the counter. That one held the clean dishes, plates, and cups. On more than one occasion, she stood on her hind legs, steadying herself by bracing her front paws on the lower shelf, to inspect the contents of that cupboard. One day, she hopped up to the shelf that held the plates and dishes. That cupboard was a bit crowded, even without a wiggly cat, which made it difficult to get a good enough grip on her to extract her. She politely complained as I set her on the floor, while I made a mental note always to close that cupboard door immediately after I was done.

Underneath the counter was a narrow cabinet for storing cookie sheets, baking pans, and similarly sized items. This opening was just a bit too narrow for Buttercup to enter for a complete inspection. Naturally, kitty wants what kitty can't have. She wasn't able to get completely inside that cabinet, but that didn't stop her from poking her head in as far as she could.

The drawers were also endlessly fascinating. I had to be quick whenever I opened one; otherwise, she'd have her paws up on its edge and would be looking down into the drawer while her mind was performing all the complex jump calculations. *Where did this space come from? Can I make it? What will I land on?* The higher the drawer, the more mysterious it was. When the top drawer containing the silverware was opened, she would stare up at it, occasionally stretching out and standing upright on her hind legs so she could get closer to the opening. To avoid the chaos that would ensue if she attempted to leap into the silverware drawer, I occasionally picked her up so she could get a better look. "See? There's nothing in there for a kitty," I would tell her. She was never quite convinced.

The door to the kitchen pantry was opened on a daily basis because that's where the cat food was stored. Normally, Buttercup and the other cats were sufficiently interested in the food that was going into their bowls or the kitty treats in my hands to stay out of the pantry. There were times, though, when that door was open and Buttercup had to explore the pantry. She could easily jump onto the first shelf, and in her younger days, she could make it to the second one. She'd check out the wares and then proudly look at me when I went to close the door. *Hey, I'm not done!*

We stored a few things on the floor of the pantry, too, including a fire extinguisher in the back corner and a large cardboard box for collecting recyclable materials. Buttercup liked to jump into that box, probably because it took up so much space that entering it was the only way to explore the rest of the ground level of the pantry.

For many years, she completely ignored the fire extinguisher. But that changed one day after I had it recharged. Upon picking it up from the service company, I noticed that they had replaced the plastic retainer that held the pull-pin in place with a different style. For some reason, Buttercup became obsessed with that piece of plastic. Once she discovered it, she became so obsessed with it that as soon as the pantry door was opened, she'd jump directly into the recycling box in order to make her way to the extinguisher and its enticing plastic loop. It must have had a nice flavor, because she wanted to bite into it. Before that, I'd normally let her explore in there all she wanted, often leaving the door open so she could satisfy her curiosity. But after she became so attracted to that piece of plastic, I started to remove her from the pantry anytime she went in there to prevent her from ingesting something she shouldn't. I discovered that the easiest way to do this was to grab the recycling container and slide it out into the kitchen, cat and all. Buttercup would give me a slightly annoyed look in return.

One cabinet in the kitchen was completely off-limits: the one directly under the sink. It housed cleaning chemicals and other things to which a cat shouldn't have access. I knew Buttercup was smart enough that she would have been OK under the sink, but I still felt better knowing that she didn't even have a chance to get into trouble. One thing this meant, though, was that I had to be very quick when accessing that cabinet.

There was only one time that she was permitted to explore that cabinet. I needed to do some plumbing work for the dishwasher, so that cabinet was going to be open much longer than normal. To make it easier for both of us, I shifted the entire contents of the cabinet to a different location for the duration of the plumbing job. That permitted me to get the job done and her to explore an otherwise forbidden place.

The cabinet under the bathroom sink was off-limits, too—well, for several years, anyway, until she eventually wore me down. Buttercup would be all over me any time I tried to restock the toilet paper that was kept there. She was so persistent that sometimes I'd have to give up halfway through the job, close the cabinet doors, and resume restocking later in the day when she was off in some other part of the house. Ultimately, she won. I'd restock while she explored, and if she ended up being in the way I would just stop and return a few minutes later.

Speaking of toilet paper, as exciting as restocking it was for Buttercup, neither she nor the other cats ever found the fun in unraveling the roll that was hung for use. Only one day did I arrive home to find a foot or so of the paper unrolled, but that was probably an accidental result of someone jumping onto the sink. I've heard stories and seen photos of cats dispersing entire rolls. Since my paper was hung in the proper overhand fashion, I always feared they might one day discover the joys that toilet paper can provide. It was actually somewhat odd that they did not play with it, especially Bubba, given his fascination with tissues.

Buttercup was also very curious about the drawers under my bed. I rarely used most of them, but one held my socks and underwear. Whenever that drawer was open, she wanted to climb into it. As I put clothes away, I normally kept that drawer closed until I had everything folded and ready to stow. I was fearful that she might crawl into drawer and then climb over the back of it, into the space behind it; I wouldn't be able to get her out, as the drawers are non-removable. Logically, there wasn't enough room back there for her to do that, plus I knew she was smart enough not to get herself into a place that she couldn't get out of, but the paranoia in me kept me from even giving her the opportunity.

Laundry, of course, could not be done without her supervision. She would dutifully follow me to the utility room in the basement where the washer and dryer were located. Surprisingly, she never jumped into either unit, although she did prop herself up to look into the dryer a few times. Of course, she'd trail me back upstairs to the bedroom and make sure that all of the clothing was folded and put away properly. Occasionally, she'd decide that I shouldn't put everything away at once; she'd stop me by jumping into the basket of freshly cleaned clothing. Her fur would inevitably end up on all of my clothing due to her lap time, but apparently, she sometimes felt the need to "pre-fur" some items. Fair enough. I'd put away what I could, sometimes sliding a few things out from under her, and then just leave the rest for later.

While doing laundry in the basement one Saturday afternoon, a slight sound caught my attention. I turned to see Buttercup chewing on the control lines for one of my radio-controlled aircraft. The airplane had been near the top of a heavy-duty shelving unit for quite some time, and I always figured the lines were safe from the cats since none had ever been able to get to that shelf. I have no idea how Buttercup managed to make her way to that shelf, but by that point, I had lived with her long enough that I was no longer surprised by her feats. When Buttercup set her mind on a goal, she accomplished it.

Although Buttercup would follow me everywhere, there were times when she'd lose interest in me. When I stayed in one place for a significant length of time, as I might do on a weekend when working on a project in the hobby room, she would perform an initial inspection of my activities, and then leave to roam her territory or take a nap. Every few hours she would check in on me, though. Sometimes this involved coming to me for some attention, but other times she would just step into the room, look at me, make sure that I saw her, and then turn around and go back to her roaming.

This connection worked both ways: If I realized that I hadn't seen her in a while, I would go looking for her.

Normally, I'd find her in the basement or plant window. Thinking back on it, I behaved the same way she did. Sometimes I'd greet her, but other times I would just confirm that she was there and then go back to what I had been doing.

The hobby room had a shallow closet with several shelves and dual sliding doors. This closet contained many things that a cat really shouldn't get into—half-finished electrical projects, boxes of parts, wires, and various tools. For several years, I kept the doors closed except when I needed to gain access to the closet. But a door, by definition, is something that a cat wants to be on the other side of. Every time I started to slide one of the doors, Buttercup would hear it. She'd come running so she could check out the mystery behind door number one. She'd inspect all of the items on the floor and then move onto the lower shelves. Some of the higher shelves could be reached with a jump, and if there appeared to be enough open space, she would take the leap. Due to the shelf layout, it was possible for a graceful cat to jump or climb some of the higher shelves. Other shelves were out of reach, but that didn't stop her from standing on her hind paws in order for a closer inspection.

That closet was to the left of the file cabinet and TV set on which she liked to climb. When I opened the door on the right side of the closet, she discovered that she could gain access to more of the shelves from the top of the file cabinet. A few times, she sneaked in so quietly I didn't even notice, only to discover her later after hearing rustling sounds from within the closet. Other times, I saw her go in but couldn't convince her to come out, so I'd just leave one of the doors open for a while so she wouldn't be trapped.

She was pretty well behaved when she examined the hobby room closet. She mostly just wanted to explore, and she rarely knocked anything over or off a shelf. The worst thing she'd do was attempt to eat the end of a wire that might be sticking out of a box or spool. I thought that perhaps if she had unlimited access to the closet, maybe it wouldn't be so mysterious and therefore it wouldn't be so tempting. As an experiment, I left the door open one time when she decided to climb around in there. The other cats generally weren't interested in getting into the closets, so it was only Buttercup that concerned me. I was still a little paranoid about her jumping between the higher shelves and the file cabinet, especially since there were parts bins stacked up outside the closet next to the cabinet. The only time she stood on those bins was when the right closet door was open, since they permitted her to get closer to the closet shelves. To prevent potential accidents with those bins, I always kept the left closet door open rather than the right. When I needed access to the right side, I'd move both doors but then move them back as soon as I was finished. As expected, once she had unlimited access to the closet there was less intrigue, so she spent much less time in there.

When I say Buttercup had to inspect everything I did, I mean *everything*. Whenever I had sinus issues due to allergies I would often use a neti pot; this is a vessel containing a warm mixture of salt water and sodium bicarbonate used to rinse and clear sinus cavities. My neti pot was made from stainless steel and normally stored out of sight in a linen closet. It was irresistible to an inquisitive cat. *Ooo! Shiny! With warm water!* But the object of using one is to get things like allergens *out* of the sinuses, not put them in, so the extra fur that came from Buttercup's curiosity was something I wanted to avoid. She liked to be on the sink while I used the device, and while she was normally well behaved, curiosity would get the best of her and she would attempt to poke her head into the neti pot. I had to place her on the floor once or twice when she disrupted my activity. Perhaps she was concerned for my safety or sanity? I can't imagine what she must have thought about what I was doing.

Buttercup would have made a wonderful library cat—she was greatly entertained by books. Or at least, book*shelves*. When she moved into the house, she discovered the built-in bookshelves in the living room, but they were not very accessible to a cat. About a year after I moved in, I rearranged the furniture, pushing the sofa against the wall with the bookshelves. The fit was perfect—the back of the sofa came right up to the bottom of the lowest shelf. Suddenly, Buttercup had several new places to explore, with walk-in access to the lowest row. The second level could be reached with a trivial jump; and with enough concentration, in her younger days she would even leap to the third set of shelves.

The shelves contained mostly books, along with a few knickknacks. The books, more or less arranged by subject, had their spines aligned with the front edge of the shelves, which created a cavity behind the row of books. Most of the shelves weren't completely full, so getting access to the space behind the books was easy. For the ones that were full, Buttercup would climb over the books to get to the hidden compartment behind them. Her attempts to get to these hidden compartments were sometimes less than graceful. One day, she was struggling to get behind the shelf of cat books when those spring-loaded claws popped out for traction, tearing the dust jacket of a book written by veterinarian Dr. Louis J Camuti. Sure, it was an accident; or, was she expressing her opinion of veterinarians in general? To prevent any further damage, I rearranged the books, leaving an opening wide enough for a cat on every shelf.

During the second half of her life, Buttercup had a fascination with water. One of the places she always had to explore was the combination bathtub and shower that I used. In the morning, she would hop up on the edge of the bathtub and slide around the shower curtain in order to jump into the tub. She'd sniff around and perhaps sample any water that happened to be pooled near the drain; apparently, my bath water has a flavor.

She had absolutely no interest in the shower curtain, but Bubba found it incredibly entertaining. He would go through periods where, for several days in a row, he'd hop into the bathtub each morning in order to play drums on the shower curtain. He'd reach as high as he could and bat at the middle of the shower curtain with his front paws. That made a nice sound, but it was just the setup. Bubba's drumming action pushed the shower curtain out slightly, making room for him on top of it. After that, he'd jump onto the edge of the tub, standing on the shower curtain so it could no longer get away from him. With the curtain now taut, he had the perfect drum that could be heard throughout the house. He'd beat that drum so hard that I figured that one day he'd pull the curtain down. So far, that hasn't happened. To Buttercup, the shower curtain wasn't a musical instrument, just a barrier in the way of a potential water source.

Sometimes Buttercup would wait for me as I took a shower, sitting on the sink and watching me through the frosted curtain. After I exited the shower, she'd jump down off the sink and make her way into the tub before I could pull the curtain closed. The bottom of the curtain would flop around a bit as I pulled it, so I figured if I tried to close it while she was wandering around in the tub, I might end up with a wet cat. Suspecting that she wouldn't like that, I would wait for her to finish whatever she needed to do before extending the curtain to let it dry out.

Sometimes she'd be done by the time I finished drying myself and was ready to leave the bathroom, but other times she wouldn't be done, so I'd just leave her to explore and hope I would remember to go back later to pull the curtain out to dry. A few times, I was able to pull the curtain out without getting her wet. That may have made it a bit more difficult for her to leave, since she'd have to go around the curtain on her way out rather than just jump straight out of the tub, but I assume she knew what she was doing. It never seemed to bother her.

Buttercup loved her windows. Windows are televisions for cats. Buttercup got to enjoy three "big-screen TVs." In the front of her house, she had the large picture window in the dining room. The kitchen featured a sliding-glass door that looked out onto the deck. A similar sliding-glass door in the basement overlooked the lattice-covered patio. I tried to position furniture such that she and the other cats would have perches adjacent to the windows that weren't close to the floor. Sometimes this was regular people furniture, other times it was purchased cat furniture, and still other times it was cat furniture that I built. Regardless, they were all heavily used.

It seemed that each window in the house had a different purpose. The large picture window in the dining room provided an excellent view of entertainment in the front yard. There were squirrels gathering nuts in the tree and birds digging up worms in the dirt. People would walk their dogs along the sidewalk and kids would ride their bikes. Occasionally, a rabbit or chipmunk would make an appearance. Buttercup was like a prairie dog at this window, resting her front paws on the sill and popping her head up in order to see what was happening outside. I eventually built a carpet-covered bench at sill height so the cats could sit or lie down while looking out the window. This window was also the primary source of morning sunshine.

After a while, I noticed this window served another purpose: It was where they sometimes waited for me to come home. As I pulled into the driveway, I would often see one or two cats sitting on the bench looking out the window toward the driveway. Not only would they watch for me when they expected me to come home, but sometimes I'd see them there when I left for work, too. They'd also use that window to keep an eye on me when I was working in the front yard.

The living room had a window that was a bit higher off the floor than the dining room window. I placed a small cat tree next to it to create another outdoor-viewing opportunity. This window provided a more relaxing and casual view, and was normally not as exciting as the view from the dining room. It also provided a great place to doze in the late afternoon sunshine. When I climbed around on the lattice roof to apply water sealer, the cats supervised me from this window.

The sliding-glass doors had very short and narrow frames, making it easy for a cat to look outside while sitting or even lying down. This window provided Buttercup with great summertime views because she could look outside and still be comfortable in the cool basement.

The cats used the glass door in the kitchen much less frequently, I think, because there was seldom anything interesting to see on the deck. Only once did Buttercup get aroused about something she saw through that glass. I poked my head around the curtain and saw a stray cat resting on the deck. Buttercup was fascinated, but did not seem overly concerned.

Large drapes covered both sets of sliding-glass doors, but a cat could easily slip between the drapes and the door for a look at nature. Buttercup did this so often that fur would build up on the backside of the drapes. The collection of fur was so great that I had to use a brush to remove it.

When the doors and windows were replaced with more energy-efficient models, both sliding-glass doors were changed to a wide French-style frame that blocked the view of any cat that chose to lie on the floor. I felt badly about taking that away from them and figured something needed to be done. I rarely used the basement door, so I decided it would be OK to put a small piece of furniture in front of it. Once again, I built a bench covered in carpet and placed it in front of the door. It was short enough that I could step over it if necessary and light enough that it could easily be moved if there wasn't a cat lying on it, or, in some cases, even if there was a cat on it. Cats love to explore nooks and crannies, so they also enjoyed the area under the new platform. Both Buttercup and Bubba liked to use the new ledge to watch the outside world.

In the small front bedroom, which I used as an office, a small table in front of the window permitted a view of the driveway. Due to the shade from a tree in the front yard and the smaller size of this window, it wasn't nearly as desirable as the one in the dining room. Like many of the other windows, this one was also used to supervise my yard work. During mild weather, I would often open this window. Buttercup enjoyed the breeze that would pass through the screen, as well as the sounds and scents of the outdoors that would waft through.

My bedroom had a window identical to the one in the office. There was no furniture that permitted the cats a good view out of this window, but they still looked up at it when they heard a bird outside in the tree. In the cooler seasons, I would open the blind to let some sunshine into the room. Buttercup enjoyed that sunbeam as she slept on the blankets.

The hobby room had two casement windows. One of them was not usable for the cats due to the furniture arrangement, but the other one was heavily used. Tables were arranged in a U-shape with the window at one corner. I made sure to keep that corner free of clutter so it was available as a feline sitting and viewing area. All of the cats used that window as I worked at the nearby computer. During the spring and fall, opening that window would permit a breeze to flow through the house. The sound of that window opening would draw cats nearly as quickly as the sound of a can opener on a can of tuna. Facing west, the hobby room window also provided plenty of afternoon sunshine. There was a toolbox near the window that I tried to keep closed because Buttercup enjoyed sleeping on it, especially when it was warmed by the sun.

The plant window in the kitchen was probably Buttercup's favorite. From a feline's perspective, it was an all-purpose window. It provided an entertaining view, a place to sleep, and plenty of sun. This metal-framed window jutted out from the house with glazing on three sides plus the top. The upper shelf was reserved for plants, while the lower shelf was available for kitties. This south-facing window was warm from spring through autumn, and even on a sunny winter day, it would heat up nicely. The window was probably original to the house, which made it fifteen years old when Buttercup moved in. Some of the seals had failed, so water would collect between the panes. In fact, there was so much dirt, grime, and mold between the panes that I had the window reglazed and sealed. After that, it looked much better and I figured the cats probably enjoyed the clearer view.

The window was double paned, but with the metal frame, it was terribly inefficient. When I replaced all of the other old windows in the house with more efficient, double-pane fiberglass windows, I left the plant window alone since I knew the cats, especially Buttercup, enjoyed sunning there.

I would often find her lying in that window when I came home from work or came inside after doing yard work. If I was working outside, I'd see her in that window napping or watching me. When she wasn't sleeping, that window was a marvelous observation point. It was fairly high and provided a near panoramic, 270-degree view. She could easily see the street, sidewalks, several of the neighbors' houses, and a small portion of the backyard. If there were exciting things to see outside—squirrels, neighbor kids, birds, rabbits—the plant window provided one of the best seats in the house. Other cats would sometimes use the window, but it was predominantly Buttercup's.

During winter nights, the plant window could get quite cold. I knew Buttercup and occasionally the other cats like to lie there, so to make it more comfortable for them I would place a bath towel on the metal base of the window. Both Buttercup and Bubba seemed to enjoy that.

The kitchen contained another front-facing window that was normally covered by blinds. That didn't stop Buttercup from getting a peek when necessary. She'd jump onto the counter next to the window and pry the blinds away with her head in order to look outside. This window was large and low enough to the floor that if she was in too big a hurry to bother with the counter, she could prop her front paws on the windowsill and poke her head through the blinds. She didn't do that on a regular basis, but only when there was something that really needed her attention, such as birds chirping in the evergreen tree just outside that window.

Buttercup definitely understood how all of these windows, taken together, provided excellent situational awareness of the world immediately outside her house. Even though she had never been outside most of the house, she knew what could be seen from each window and where the views overlapped. If something exciting were happening outside, such as a rabbit running across the yard, she would run from one window to the next to follow the action. She'd even run from one floor of the house to the other in order to get a better view. Some days I had no idea what she saw that got her so worked up; I'd try to check, but by the time I got to the window, whatever she'd seen was gone.

Others noticed Buttercup's propensity for quick action. Visitors mentioned how Buttercup was always in motion. She would endlessly patrol her territory, keeping an eye on the other cats, activity outside the windows, and of course, me. If she and I were in the same room, she would always be in motion, inspecting everything regardless of how many times or how recently she had inspected it. Even when she decided to settle down for a while on my lap, the tip of her tail would keep moving, gently swaying back and forth, while her radar-like ears kept her alert to her environment.

Tabbies on a Table

Chapter 13: Unquestioned Love

One of the greatest benefits of living with a pet is the consistent and nonjudgmental companionship. A cat isn't concerned about financial status or material goods; if someone provides an understanding, loving, and caring home for her, she will return that affection tenfold. This was never truer than with Buttercup.

Buttercup always greeted me at the door when I came home from work. I wondered if she was running on her internal clock, or if she picked up on some other cue, such as the sound of the garage door opening, to know when to make her way to the door. When my schedule varied, it became clear: she was picking up on sounds *and* expecting me home at a specific time. If I arrived home early or stopped by during the day, she typically was not at the door when I opened it, but would soon make her way there. She'd give me an inquisitive look. *You're home early. What's going on?* But when I arrived home late, I received a very different treatment. She'd be at the door giving me a terribly nasty look. *Where have you been?! I've been worried sick!*

In her later years, she let the younger cats trip me at the door while she waited patiently at the top of the half-flight of stairs. After walking through the doorway and stopping briefly to greet Lily, I would take a step or two up and then lean over to pet Buttercup. She'd often greet me with a soft *meow* and then immediately turn around, letting my hand rub the side of her head and her back. When she did this, she'd turn around completely, but not before pausing briefly halfway through the turn. She'd sometimes do this turn-and-pause routine when she walked on my lap, too. That is, she'd basically shove her butt in my face. I tried to tell her that despite it being a normal form of interaction with other cats, I really had no need or desire to smell her behind. As often as I told her that, however, she never stopped this behavior with me. Perhaps she did this because she had long ago accepted me into her feline society.

Buttercup liked to use the "hover cat" pose for napping—lowering her body onto all four, retracted paws. This was the pose that cartoonist Bernard Kliban once said looks like a meatloaf with a long tail and triangular ears. When Buttercup really wanted to settle in for a nap, she would wrap her tail around the left side of her body—always the left side. She must have felt it was more comfortable to wrap her tail to the left, just as I generally find sleeping on my left side is more desirable than sleeping on my right.

When she lay on my lap, she would do the same thing with her tail, but as she aged, I noticed that she would do it less often. Perhaps it was due to the arthritis that developed during her last couple of years. If she was on my lap and seemed like she was going to settle in for a while, I would gently take her tail and lay it next to the left side of her body. Sometimes it would flop back down, but often it would stay in place. She seemed to appreciate that.

Buttercup liked to sleep on my lap anytime and anywhere she could get to it. A couple of the more common places were on the sofa in the living room and on a chair in the hobby room. If she weren't in the mood to lie down right away, she would often sit on my pelvis, facing me. She would knead my stomach with both front paws, practically until I was sick. As she did this, I would stroke her back with both hands, sometimes synchronized with her kneading. This synchronized petting would probably have looked pretty funny to anyone who saw us. Her eyelids would start to close as she softly purred with contentment.

After a while, she would stop the kneading and curl up on my lap for a long nap.

Often, lying on my lap wasn't enough "touch" for her—she wanted my hand, too. Whenever she sat or lay on my lap, I would pet or massage her. With my left hand, I would gently scratch her neck—an action that she responded to so well that even the doctors at the Cat Clinic would use it to help keep her happy during examinations. After several minutes of neck massage, she was ready for a nap and would demand the use of my left hand for her pillow. She would rest her chin on my hand and place her front left paw on the back of my wrist. Sometimes I would continue to stroke her softly from her head to mid-back with my free hand as she dozed off into a blissful kitty sleep.

If she were on my lap and not receiving a neck massage, typically because I was busy working on something, she would motion for my left hand. She would raise the front half of her body enough that she could reach for my front left paw with her front left paw. As soon as I put my hand down where she wanted it, she was happy. She would hold it down with her paw and then place her head on my hand. I'm not sure if she did this for comfort or if it was an issue of control—whoever has her paw on top is the more dominant one, and in this case Buttercup's was always on top.

Bubba had a similar paw-on-paw behavior with me when he'd lie down on the bed at night. He'd always lie near the pillow on whichever side I was facing. He'd put one or both of his front paws on my arm, and I'd always respond by placing a hand on one or both of his paws. Usually within minutes—sometimes seconds—he'd pull one of his paws out and either place it on top of mine or move it next to mine. He'd sometimes do that with his other paw, too, but unlike Buttercup, he frequently let me hold his paw down. Sometimes I'd lightly squeeze his paw and he'd respond by squeezing back. Bubba's actions are further evidence that the paw-on-paw behavior relates to dominance; I outranked Bubba so he permitted me to hold his paw, but Buttercup clearly outranked me and therefore demanded to have her paw on top.

Some of my most cherished memories of Buttercup are of the close interaction that we had. When she lay on a table or the floor, I would offer her my hand. With my palm exposed, I'd cup my fingers slightly. She would softly rest her head on my palm and leave it there long after my hand ached due to the lack of support. It was so nice to know that she trusted me enough to do that.

Ironically, if I attempted to lie down on the floor near her, she would often get up. Despite all of the lap time and snuggling on the sofa and bed, if I attempted to initiate something like that, she rarely wanted anything to do with it. If I lay on the floor, she rarely lay down with me. In fact, I only remember one time when she lay down near me and put her head on one of my legs.

There was one thing she frequently did when I was on the floor. Even though she didn't want to cuddle with me there, that didn't mean we had no physical interaction.

If I was on the floor, typically playing with one of the cats, she'd investigate what I was doing and frequently, she'd walk across me. Was that another sign of her dominance over me?

🐾 🐾 🐾

Tails are an outlet for the expression of emotion for many animals. You can tell a lot about how a cat is feeling by observing his or her tail. When Lily felt playful, she would lie with her body flat to the ground and her head raised. Her feather-duster-like tail would swoosh back and forth behind her.

Bubba's long, thin tail would hang down with a slight curl so that it didn't brush the floor as he walked. If I called him from the other side of the room, he would perk up and perhaps reply with his trademark squeak. As he trotted toward me, his tail would be straight up in the air. His tail was in continuous motion with fast, unpredictable, jerking movements that matched his skittish personality perfectly.

At the other end of the spectrum, Buttercup's tail expressed her quiet confidence. As she sat to observe the world around her, her tail wouldn't be straight out or wrapped up around her as when she napped, but off to one side with a slight curl. The tip was endlessly in motion with a slight and soft twitch.

There were private times, though, when Buttercup's tail expressed more personal and intimate feelings. When I sat on the steps at the doorway to the garage to put my shoes on, Buttercup would often be there, wanting to socialize. If she jumped onto my lap, she would often wrap her tail around me. From butt to tip, she would softly rub her whole tail against my side and back. She would also do this when I was standing at the bathroom sink. After jumping onto the sink, she'd find herself at the perfect height to display this affection toward me, wrapping her tail around my midsection.

She would do other things to show affection for me, too. Some researchers believe that when a cat rubs the side of her head on an object she is using scent glands in that part of her body to mark that object as being part of her territory. They say, though, that rubbing the top of her head against someone (human or another cat) is a display of affection. Based on my fourteen years with Buttercup, I believe they are correct. She would often brush the top of her head against me. She would even walk around on my lap and shove the top of her head under my arm. If the girl has her head buried in your armpit, the seduction period is over; you can rest assured that she likes you.

Buttercup would also rub the top of her head against Bubba's head. She may have been dominant over him, but she also cared for him.

Bubba, being a much manlier cat, kept his head out of my armpits, but he did show similar behavior with the way he rubbed the top of his head against other parts of my body. I could often hold my hand out to him and he'd walk up to it, lower his head, and brush the top of his head against my fingers. He'd do that even when I didn't motion toward him. Frequently when I used the computer, he'd walk in front of me and lower his head in order to pry my hand up over it. He seemed to believe that the primary purpose of human hands was to pet cats.

Here's something I've always wondered: if rubbing the side of her head on something was Buttercup's way of declaring that object to be hers, what did it mean when I scratched the side of her head? Was I basically telling her that I belonged to her? Is that how she came to be the dominant leader of my household?

In the summer of 2009, I began volunteering once a week at an all-cat animal shelter. I wasn't sure how this would go over with my feline family, since I would come home smelling of other cats. To cut down on the chances of spreading kitty colds between them and the cats at the shelter, I would always start a load of laundry with my dirty clothes as soon as I got home, in addition to washing myself thoroughly. The cats knew, though. The first few weeks, they sniffed me over pretty well after I arrived home but soon it didn't bother them. I'd like to think that they understood that I was helping less fortunate kitties that didn't yet have *fur*-ever homes. Buttercup was a compassionate cat whom the others looked up to; perhaps she let the others know that my activities were acceptable.

Another excellent example of Buttercup's compassion was the way she shared my lap with other cats. Lily was never really a lap cat, so there wasn't an issue when she moved in. Bubba liked lap time, but was easily excitable and wouldn't stick around very long. Still, there were times when he wanted to be on my lap or held in my arms. Usually Buttercup was already on my lap, so when Bubba showed up, he would try to wedge his way in. He was very respectful of Buttercup and wouldn't try to take my lap away from her. Rather, he'd climb onto my arms so I'd end up with one cat on my lap and one in my arms. Occasionally, Bubba would readjust his position, unknowingly crowding Buttercup. She was quite accepting of this. Sometimes she didn't seem bothered by it, but other times she would decide to get up and leave for a while.

There were times, though, when Bubba showed up first and decided to lie on my lap. Buttercup would then arrive and look around. If Bubba were there, she would occasionally lie on my legs if my feet were up or resting on a chair, but normally she would decide to not bother Bubba or me and would come back later. She knew that Bubba normally didn't stay on my lap very long.

The two tabbies eventually came to a lap-sharing agreement. When I was on the chair in the hobby room, it seemed my lap was almost never without a cat. Buttercup would jump up and spend a good amount of time there, as usual. But when she got down, it would only be a minute or two before Bubba showed up for his turn. He wouldn't stick around as long as Buttercup did, and minutes after he jumped down, Buttercup would be back for her next round. It would go on and on like this all evening. On the weekends, it might go on and on all afternoon *and* evening. I learned that if I needed to get up for something I had to do it immediately after a cat jumped off my lap, otherwise there might not be another chance for quite some time.

🐾 🐾 🐾

Soon after Lily moved in, but long before Bubba was on the scene, another male cat lived with us for a while. Norm, a coworker who lived with five cats, was planning to take a job outside the country. He could take the cats with him, but they would have to be quarantined for six months before moving to their new home. He didn't want to put them or himself through that, so he decided to find loving homes for them in this country. After hearing that I lived with two girls, he thought Booger might be a good fit. I couldn't stand the thought of calling a cat "Booger," so he became "Bogie" when he moved in. Bogie was a large black-and-white tuxedo cat with a very friendly demeanor and calm temperament. His hobbies were lap time and being lazy. Due to his sheer size, he was an ominous presence in any room he entered, but he was quite polite and accepting of the girls.

Lily seemed to enjoy having another playmate. Buttercup was accepting of Bogie, too, but I don't think she was all that happy about having him in the house. She could have been more assertive with him, as she was later with Bubba, but I think she was a bit intimidated by his size, even though he was never aggressive toward either of the girls. When Bogie moved in, he chose to sleep on the bed with me. During this time, Buttercup stopped sleeping on the bed. She would prop herself up on the edge of the bed with her front paws and take a look. If Bogie were there, she would leave the room.

When Bogie moved in, he brought a small cat tree with him. He would jump up to the top, V-shaped platform and lie there even if Buttercup was already there. She would politely stand her ground but seemed a bit annoyed by him, possibly because he didn't even notice he was crowding her.

Bogie didn't stay with us very long. Norm's new job fell through, so he ended up staying in this country. Without Booger things didn't seem quite right at his house, so Booger gave up his Bogie persona and went back to live with Norm and his four other feline roommates. Norm reported that he readjusted instantly to living with his old family. To Booger, it was just a month-long vacation with a couple of nice female kitties. Buttercup seemed happier after he left and immediately started sleeping in my bed again.

Buttercup was apparently a believer in President Theodore Roosevelt's "Speak softly and carry a big stick" philosophy. She rarely raised her voice with the other cats, yet they knew she meant business. They knew Buttercup was capable of maintaining strict discipline in her house. They may have occasionally become playful with her, but they were never insolent.

She was soft-spoken with me, too. She knew how to get my attention if I wasn't in the room, although she rarely had a need to do that. When she was near, she rarely spoke, but when she did, it was almost a whisper of a meow. Sometimes her mouth would open, but no sound would come out. When she spoke to me, I would answer her back. We may have spoken different languages, but we always seemed to understand each other clearly. By the way she looked at me, she seemed to know that I understood every word she meowed.

Anyone who says cats are solitary creatures has just never taken the time to get to know one. They may not always interact with each other in noticeable ways, but they certainly vie for their human's time. This was apparent when Buttercup first moved in. She would patrol and monitor her house, but she'd always end up in whichever room I was occupying. Even when she was entertaining herself with her toys, she preferred to be near me. Over the years, some of her behaviors and habits would vary, but one thing that never did was her desire to be close to me, be it lying on the floor or on the table near me, or on my lap, or curled up next to me at night.

Lily, too, was always social. First, she was a talkative kitty. She'd walk into the room, take a seat, and then as soon as I looked at her she'd start telling me all about her day. She liked to be close, too. I discovered quite by accident one day that she would spoon with me. If I lay down on my side on the floor near her, she would immediately get up, walk over to me, lie down by my chest, and rest her head on my arm. She liked to do that on the sofa, too. Interestingly enough, she would never spoon with me on the bed. Rather, her bedroom social activities centered on repeatedly walking across my chest in the morning, letting me know that it was time for breakfast. Only when she realized that I wasn't going to fall for it would she lie down next to or on top of me, and then usually only for a short period.

Bubba also had some interesting ways of interacting. As a kitten, he wasn't much of a lap cat, at least with me. One evening while my parents were visiting, he was resting on top of the small cat tree by the window, exhausted after a day of playing. After about an hour of sleeping curled in a ball on the cat tree, he awoke, stood up, stretched, and jumped from his perch. Very deliberately, as if on a mission, he walked across the room to the sofa where my parents were seated. He walked under my mother's legs and then jumped onto a small open spot on the cushion between my parents. Without stopping, he stepped onto my mother's lap, circled once, and lay down for another nap. Although he had just met her a day or two before, he knew that Grandma was for cuddling.

As he grew, he became more of a lap cat with me. He was so active and jumpy that normally he'd just pass through my lap for a few seconds. Unlike Buttercup, he wouldn't sleep on my lap for hours. And, of course, any time he was on my lap it had to be *his* idea. I could pick him up, but within seconds, he would fight to get down. Since he recognized me as the alpha male, he tolerated me, but it was obvious he wanted to get away.

One day I performed an experiment. I picked him up and cradled him close to me. He was very tense, but I remained calm and continued to hold him firmly for a while. Sometime during that event, his attitude changed completely. I relaxed my grip and then couldn't get rid of him! Without being restrained at all, he readjusted his position on my chest and stayed there for quite some time. Soon after that, he would eagerly get onto my lap or crawl into my arms of his own free will. One of his adorable traits was the way he expressed affection while on my lap. He'd stand close to me and then push the whole side of his body from head to tail into my chest. He never accomplished the full tail-wrap that Buttercup would do, but like her, he would look up at me affectionately.

Compared to Buttercup's calm confidence, Bubba was always quite apprehensive and jittery. He frequently seemed rather tense, and only rarely would he relax. Even when he seemed very at ease, if I made even a slight movement, he would bolt. If he was resting on the chair next to me, seconds later he might be flying down the hall, only to return a moment later, once he realized all was safe. That behavior was funny, except when he used my stomach as his springboard. Interestingly, it seemed as though when he was on *my* chair he became much more composed and therefore less likely to give up his spot.

Unlike Buttercup, who was known to ignore my dates or visitors, Bubba was always cautious and uneasy when strangers were in the house. One woman had only seen Bubba from a distance when she visited me, so one evening when Bubba finally worked up the courage to approach her, she turned to look at me and gasped with delight. That sound was all it took to undo the courage Bubba had worked up; he immediately fled, and I don't think she ever saw him again.

Even when I approached him, Bubba would often quickly shuffle away as if he was trying to keep me from getting close enough to pick him up. But there's no understanding a cat's behavior—sometimes he'd do the complete opposite. If I walked toward him, occasionally he'd slowly roll head first to the floor, exposing his belly to me. That seemed to be the sign that he wanted his belly rubbed. As I gave him a belly rub, he'd roll onto his back and softly talk to me.

Whenever I took a bath, all of the cats would stop by to check up on me. I would temporarily place a folding chair in the bathroom to use as a table for things like a book, magazine, snack, or drink. This backfired, though, when Bubba decided that he needed to lie on the chair in order to keep tabs on me. Once on the chair, he was there for the duration. If he got up, it was only to briefly get a drink of my bathwater. Fortunately, he was very graceful and careful around the potentially wet bathtub rim; only once did he fall in. Not wanting a wet cat, I instinctively raised my left leg to catch him. Everything happened so fast that even as my leg was going up, my mind hadn't completely processed the thought that what I was doing was quite dangerous; I could have ended up with a shredded leg. Fortunately, Bubba always had excellent self-control with his claws. Unlike Buttercup, I can't remember a single incident when I ever felt Bubba's claws on my skin. Even as his paws hit the water, his claws remained retracted. With the help of my leg, he was able to work his way back up and out of the tub. I hopped out to help dry him off—I think that was the only time he ever hissed at me. I backed down and let him be, figuring he knew what he was doing. I also figured I'd never see him in the bathroom again, but a few minutes later, he shrugged off the whole experience and was back on his chair perch napping and watching over me.

Buttercup would rarely get on the chair, but she would often be in the bathroom to keep an eye on me. She would lie down on the bathroom floor and catnap on the rug or, more often, on my towel. Occasionally, she'd jump up onto the edge of the bathtub. One incident was quite memorable. The story actually started before she moved in with me on a cool day in December 1998. The day before I went to pick her up, I began to feel sick. It seemed like a minor sinus issue or the common cold, and I figured it would pass quickly. My throat was sore but I felt well enough to call Marty to see if Buttercup was still available. She was, so I went over to get her. As the weeks passed and Buttercup adjusted to her new house, my illness became worse. Soon it was apparent that I had some type of flu. By the third week of January, I felt absolutely awful. I had practically every symptom imaginable and was drained of energy. I missed an entire week of work due to that illness. At one point during that week, I decided to take a long, hot bath. During my bath, Buttercup came in to the bathroom. She jumped onto the edge of the bathtub and lay down facing me. As I soaked in misery, she stayed with me, doing what she could to comfort me. She was there for me.

Nearly fourteen years later, in September 2012, she was the one who was sick. Earlier in the year, she had been diagnosed with preliminary kidney failure. She had been losing weight and was receiving fluids three days a week. During her treatment, she did quite well. Her authority as queen of the house was never questioned. But she continued to lose weight and eventually started to lose strength. Finally came a Wednesday night that I knew would be her last. She had been crying and was cold. I could tell she was hurting. I spent the whole night with her, catnapping when she did. I held her in my arms when she would let me. When she wanted to lie on the floor, I lay down next to her and covered her with a towel to help keep her warm.

Lily and Bubba checked up on us throughout the night. They knew something wasn't right. As Buttercup was slipping away from me, I recalled the evening that she spent by my side on the edge of the bathtub when I was wasn't feeling well. Now she was the one who wasn't feeling well and it was time for me to return the favor. I spent the entire night with her, trying to keep her warm, comforting her, telling her I loved her, and just being there for her so she knew she wasn't alone. I thought back about all the years we'd spent together. I reminisced about her loving nature and her hilarious antics, like getting her paws wet while grabbing the water dish before I could even finish filling it; she left many paw prints on the sink, the counter, and the table. She left paw prints everywhere! But she left even more on my heart.

Epilogue

There have been reports about people experiencing encounters with loved ones after they depart. In some cases, people report seeing or at least feeling the presence of departed pets, too. Nothing like that has happened to me, except maybe once. On the day of Buttercup's passing, she received a private cremation service. The service was performed early in the afternoon and was done by 2:00 p.m. Given the events of that day, I hadn't had any appetite all morning and hadn't had anything to eat, so on the way home from the crematorium, I figured I needed to find some lunch. Not being in the mood to prepare a meal, I decided to go through a McDonald's drive-through. Buttercup's urn was resting on the passenger seat. Some people may have thought it was odd or creepy, but I figured it wasn't the first time she'd gone through a drive-through with me.

Upon arriving home, I took my normal spot on the sofa. Lily sat on the coffee table in front of me and waited patiently for her bite. Had Buttercup still been with me, she would have been by my side and quite a bit more aggressive than Lily was, possibly even climbing on me and grabbing for the food. As I unwrapped my cheeseburger, I briefly felt something on the cushion next to my right leg. It felt as though a couple of small paws had stepped onto the cushion. It happened very quickly. Was it a muscle spasm? Was it Buttercup letting me know she was OK? I couldn't see anything out of the ordinary, but I definitely felt something, and it was enough to make me pause. For a few seconds, I stared at my meal thinking, *If I see a tiny bite disappear from this cheeseburger...* Then I couldn't help but chuckle at how cartoonish that would be, but it would have been *so* like her to go after my cheeseburger. Then I found myself inexplicably moving my right hand as if I were petting her.

In the weeks after Buttercup's passing, the other cats in my life spent more time with me. Lily had always spent very little time on my lap, but after Buttercup was gone, she sought out my lap almost daily. Was she mourning for her friend? Was she doing that to comfort me? Or had she been a lap cat all along and was happy that she could now get access to my lap? Or perhaps she decided that she was now the dominant female of the house and was taking over Buttercup's former responsibilities? It did seem like she spent more time inspecting and supervising my activities. At times, it seemed like she was *trying* to be the alpha female, but it conflicted with her lack of desire to be a lap cat. She would walk on the table between the computer screen and me, and then act as if she wanted lap time. But once her front paws were on my leg, she would freeze. *Need to be the leader, but I don't want to sit on a lap. What do I do?!*

Lily also started howling. She'd rarely do it when I was in the room, but she'd go to the other end of the house and meow loudly, even in the middle of the night. Was she looking for her friend, as Buttercup had cried for her friends after she moved in with me?

Bubba changed a bit, too. In addition to spending more time with me, he took over the spot on the bed that Buttercup had used, at least when I was not sleeping. Once I got into bed, he reverted to the location that he had chosen over three years earlier—near the pillow next to my head on whichever side of the bed I was facing.

Perhaps this behavior was just them—and me—adjusting to the hierarchical change. Everyone moved up a slot! With Buttercup gone, I was once again at the top, followed by Bubba, and then Lily. Things were definitely different. It took some time for all of us to get used to our new positions.

My time with Buttercup is something I'll never forget. There will be more cats in my life; there may even be another brown/silver mackerel tabby. But there will never be another Buttercup.

Acknowledgments

Many individuals and organizations have influenced my life in one way or another, leading to this project. I would like to offer thanks:

To the current and former doctors at the Cat Clinic of Johnson County, for the wonderful care they provided to Buttercup during the last fourteen years of her life, including owner (at the time) Dr. Irene Schomacker, and Dr. Natasha "Tash" Taylor (current practice owner), Dr. Bonnie DeChant, and Dr. Tara Culley. I would also like to thank the veterinary technicians, staff, and feline employees at the Cat Clinic who oversaw Buttercup's care, including Wendy, Terra, Emily, DeWayne, Gabrielle, Kayla, Sara, Cheryl, Sassy, Ophelia, and Blackster. The Cat Clinic made a generous monetary contribution to the College of Veterinary Medicine at Kansas State University in memory of Buttercup. With this gift, Buttercup lives on to help make a difference in the lives of countless other animals.

To Don and Marty Mather for bringing Buttercup into my life and for providing a feline resort for her when I traveled out of town. Buttercup always did well when she visited her old home, but Lily had trouble while at this strange house. I don't think Lily realized just what a great place it was. Despite the trying times that Lily created, the Mathers were always gracious and patient with her.

To Anne Smith and the staff at The Amos Family Pet Companion Crematory run by The Amos Family Funeral Home. Their sensitivity and understanding were instrumental in making a very difficult day of my life manageable. They also created a clay cast of Buttercup's paw print. The paw print that appears in the epilogue is based on a scan of that clay casting. Scaled versions of Buttercup's paw print are used for the section delineators and on the spine.

To Elaine Doran, the founder and president of Purrfect Pets Cat Adoption, a 501(c) (3) nonprofit humane organization. Elaine understands cats better than anyone I know and makes sure all cats that come to the shelter get the absolute best care possible before they go to their *fur*-ever homes, and takes the time to make sure each and every cat is matched up with a human who will continue to provide wonderful care.

To Purrfect Pets volunteers Jen Zaman and Paula Hayek. Jen reviewed an early, very rough draft of my manuscript, and Paula reviewed an early draft of the cover.

To Tommy Short for providing feedback and guidance on the design of the cover, and Aaron Gerber for additional help with the cover.

To Lora Cox for reviewing both the manuscript and the cover.

To Darek Benesh for reviewing the manuscript.

To Zac Hester for providing design assistance and hosting for Buttercup's website, legendarybuttercup.com.

To my parents, for providing a life with animals that permitted me to experience the incredible joy of developing a human/animal bond. While growing up, my family shared our house with multiple animals over the years, including cats, dogs, gerbils, and a rabbit. I can't imagine what life would be like without animal companionship.

Finally, I would like to thank my dear Buttercup for her help in raising Lily and Bubba from kittens to the wonderful cats that they became, for being next to me when I fell asleep, for being next to me when I awoke, and for the nearly fourteen years of unquestioned love, understanding, entertainment, affection, and companionship that she gave me. I love you, Buttercup.

About the Author

Jerome Tonneson has spent twenty years in the aviation industry as an electrical and software engineer. He has worked on satellite communication systems, transponders, traffic awareness systems, navigation radios, and flight controls. Outside of work, recreational cycling and technical hobbies involving amateur radio, electronics, high-power rocketry, or any mix thereof, occupy his time. He also spends time metalworking, maintaining his acreage, designing and building cat furniture, and volunteering at a no-kill, non-profit, all-volunteer, all-cat animal shelter. This is his first book.

www.ingramcontent.com/pod-product-compliance
Lightning Source LLC
Chambersburg PA
CBHW022357040426
42450CB00005B/222